NATURAL HISTORY COLLECTOR:

Hunt, Discover, Learn!

NATURAL HISTORY COLLECTOR:

Hunt, Discover, Learn!

Expert tips on how to care for and display your collections and turn your room into a cabinet of curiosities

MICHAEL SANCHEZ

of the New Mexico Museum of Natural History and Science

QUARRY

CONTENTS

COLLECTING ROCKS AND MINERALS

COLLECTING ANIMAL AND BIRD TRACKS

COLLECTING SEASHELLS

COLLECTING FOSSILS

COLLECTING INSECTS

COLLECTING PLANTS

INTRODUCTION

If you're looking through the pages of this book, then you probably have a few treasures from the woods, the beach, or the backyard displayed on your bedroom shelves. Perhaps you already think of yourself as a collector—and you probably *are* one if you're that curious about nature and all its wonders. So, welcome, this book is for you.

Natural history collections often begin with a single object that catches your eye. It might be an interesting rock, a fossil, or an iridescent shell. Perhaps you take it home and try to find out more about it. Or maybe you just keep it on your desk where you can look at it and marvel at the way nature works. Then the next time you're out for a walk you find another example—only it's different from the first. You begin noticing things: that some of the pebbles you pick up are striped with color and some sparkle in the sun, that you can find a single type of seashell in an amazing range of sizes, that there are many kinds of animal tracks left overnight in the snow.

Once you start noticing those things it's hard to stop. It's exciting. It can also be the beginning of an amazing adventure that develops into a passion and a desire to learn more. This book will take you to the next stage of your discovery process—knowing what to do with your treasures after you bring them home. Depending on whether you're interested in plants, shells, rocks, or other things you discover, the following chapters will help you learn how to clean, store, and display your specimens.

We'll give you tips on how to keep track of your collection by keeping a notebook—so that your knowledge of your subject builds on your own discoveries. And we'll tell you about some interesting people who were young natural history collectors like you.

In the years that I've worked at the New Mexico Museum of Natural History and Science, I've had the opportunity to talk to many children who maintain a collection. What I love best about discussing their collections with them is discovering how each one has learned to speak with authority and become an expert on his or her chosen subject. The same will be true for you. As your collection grows, so will your knowledge, your vocabulary, and your confidence.

—*Michael Sanchez*

CURIOUSER AND CURIOUSER

This book promises to teach you how to turn your room into a cabinet of curiosities. Find out why.

Curiosity: from Latin, *curiosus*, inquisitive
Curator: from Latin, *curare*, to take care of

Four hundred years ago there were no public museums for families or school groups to visit. But in Europe, people were beginning to get excited about the voyages of discovery being made by explorers. Perhaps even more exciting were the wondrous natural specimens from the plant, mineral, and animal worlds that sailors and scientists brought back from their voyages to distant parts of the globe.

People with an interest in science and learning often set aside a cabinet, or a whole room, in their house for displaying their collection of exotic "curiosities." These might be anything from ostrich eggs, hummingbird bones, and shark teeth, to geodes, hairy spiders, and pineapples. People in the 1600s weren't necessarily knowledgeable about the things in their collections, but they were interested in learning. *Curiosity* comes from the Latin word for "inquisitive," and that's the start of being a collector and curator.

When they were shared with friends and other collectors, the cabinets of curiosities in people's homes became the first natural history museums. We'll show you how to turn your room into a cabinet of curiosities with projects and suggestions for cataloging, mounting, and displaying your collections.

A COLLECTION NEEDS A CURATOR

At a museum of natural history, a curator is an expert in a chosen subject—rocks, minerals, fossils, plants, shells—whatever his or her interest might be. In a large museum, with many staff members, a curator might have a single focused specialty, and in a small museum, with a small staff, a curator might have several overlapping specialties. If you've ever attended a museum's "Identification Day," when you can bring in the things you've found and have your questions answered, then you've already met a curator or two.

A collection can begin with someone being curious about one thing and then grow in all directions. Each area of natural history is huge, whether you are interested in bugs, rocks, shells, plants, or fossils.
Scientist at work, entomologist studying beetle specimens at the Natural History Museum, London, UK. Bridgeman Images. NHM1454919

The owner of these "curiosities" was so proud of his collection that he had an artist paint a picture of it. Along with corals and insects, the collection includes mirrors and scientific instruments, which were also rare in the 1600s. *Cabinet of Curiosities* (with glass doors), by Andrea Dominico Remps (1621–1699). / De Agostini Picture Library / G. Nimatallah / Bridgeman Images DGA511189

Curators' careers might start with a curiosity about nature when they're children, and, like you, an interest in collecting things and learning more about them. In high school, they discover a deeper interest when they take science classes. And then in college, they'll specialize in a subject area such as geology (rocks and minerals), botany (plants), zoology (animals), marine biology (sea life), entomology (insects), or paleontology (fossils) to develop their expertise. There are also many experts who become good at what they do simply because they have a passion for learning about their subject: There is a world authority on a particular type of beetle at our museum of natural history. But he didn't train to be an entomologist—he's a retired chemist!

Becoming an expert doesn't really ever stop. One of the exciting things about being a curator is that you keep looking and learning every day. Sometimes that may involve field research, such as hunting for dinosaur bones in the Gobi desert or studying rare plants in the Brazilian rain forest. Sometimes it involves identification of species and understanding the differences between them, such as discovering the differences and similarities among the hundreds of types of ants in the world. Sometimes it involves taking care of rare or one-of-a-kind specimens and knowing how to protect them and how to display them.

You can bring all those skills to your own collection, as you research, identify, and conserve your treasures. If you want to develop your skills further, many natural history museums offer classes and workshops. Nature centers and scouting programs are also great for getting started.

KEEPING TRACK OF YOUR COLLECTION

HOW TO START AND KEEP A FIELD NOTEBOOK

One of the best ways to practice your curatorial skills is to keep a field notebook where you can write down your observations of nature and the specimens you collect. Of course, you can keep track of your field notes and photos digitally, but you might find it particularly satisfying to maintain your records in a binder. (Or if you collect several different types of things—like plants and rocks—you might want a separate binder for each!)

There's definitely something special about being able to sit at your desk and page through a book about your favorite subject that you've written and illustrated yourself. If you also jot down notes about some of the adventures you experience on your collecting forays, the book will double as a journal of where you've been, what you've done, and when it happened.

Although any kind of notebook will work, a three-ring binder is especially useful. Many have plastic covers that can be wiped clean and the binder will allow you to remove pages and add new ones. Because they are available in many thicknesses, you can keep a thin one in your backpack and then transfer the day's pages to a thicker binder when you get home.

On a visit to a stationary or art supply shop—in person or online—you'll discover that there are many useful inserts available for a collector's notebook. There's lined paper for notes, of course, plain paper for drawings and sketches, graph paper for charts, and tabbed dividers to mark the different sections. All of these are available with the holes pre-punched.

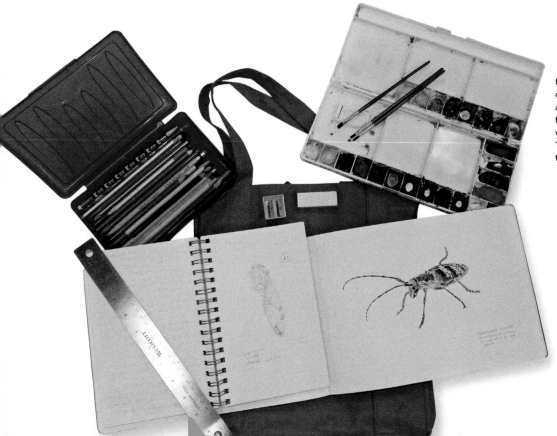

Making drawings of specimens on-site, and then finishing them at home, will help train your eye to observe nature closely—and will polish up your drawing skills! This is my quick-grab kit, ready to go when I am.

A Little Bit About Scientific Names

Through the years there have been many schemes for classifying living things. The Greek philosopher Aristotle (384–322 BCE) divided animals from plants and then animals with blood from those without blood. He also grouped animals by the way they moved—if they flew, swam, or walked. Aristotle's system was used until the 1600s!

In 1753, a Swedish scientist named Carl Linnaeus (1707–1778) developed a system called "binomial (*bi* = two, *nomial* = name) classification." In his system, every living thing has two names: the first name is the genus or group name that pulls together similar organisms. For instance, animals that look like dogs are all in the genus *Canis*, and most small cats are in the genus *Felis*.

The second name is the species name, so dogs are *Canis familiaris* (Latin for "dog-familiar") and wolves are *Canis lupus* (Latin for "dog-wolf.") House cats are *Felis catus* (cat-cat) and wild cats are *Felis silvestris* (cat-wild). *Tyrannosaurus rex* means "tyrant lizard king." Notice that the genus is always capitalized, and the species name is always lowercase. Scientific names are always set apart from other text by being italicized (or sometimes by being underlined).

Scientific names are important so that people everywhere know that they are all talking about the same thing. The common names for things in nature are different in every language. Herring gulls are *gaviota* in Spanish, *mouette* in French, and *möwe* in German. But their scientific name, *Larus argentatus*, is the same everywhere in the world!

Does the pattern on this shell look like musical notes to you? It did to Carl Linnaeus, who, in 1758, named this shell *Voluta musica*—the music volute.

But there are *other* three-hole supplies, too. These include zip-closed plastic pouches, which are perfect for carrying your colored pens and pencils, or for keeping a supply of paper towels or tissue paper handy when you need to carry small and delicate specimens. You can also transport plants, leaves, and small shells and rocks in zip-closed pouch.

You'll also find clear plastic sleeves, which come in many styles. They are the size of an 8½ x 11-inch (21.5 x 28 cm) sheet of paper, but are divided into pockets of different sizes to hold photos, postcards, or full sheets of paper. The latter can be useful, for instance, if you keep an identification guide or an animal track chart in your notebook and want to protect it so that it doesn't become beat up with use.

With the three-ring binder, you will be able to move all of the components around in the notebook, so that your observational drawings appear where you want them, and you can compare photos and notes from different days.

These field notebooks were started back in 2009 when the collector was still in school. They are just as useful today. Plastic sleeves in a binder keep photos, drawings, and notes protected. A hardcover journal is perfect for pressing leaves and making drawings. Decorate the covers of your notebooks any way you like.

Taxonomy and How Dear King Philip Came Over For Good Soup

Taxonomy is the study of how living things are related to each other and then classified. We use eight levels of classification for every living thing: Domain, Kingdom, Phylum, Class, Order, Family, Genus, and Species. The classifications get more and more specific as you go down the list. The mnemonic (reminding device) "**D**ear **K**ing **P**hilip **C**ame **O**ver **F**or **G**ood **S**oup" will help you remember the right order for the list.

Let's see how domestic dogs are classified:

DOMAIN	Eukariota	Organisms with cells with a nucleus vs. cells without (like bacteria)
KINGDOM	Animalia	Animals, as compared to land plants, fungi, and slime molds
PHYLUM	Chordata	Animals with a backbone
CLASS	Mammalia	Animals with a backbone, warm blood, fur, and skin glands
ORDER	Carnivora	Mammals that mostly eat meat, such as bears, cats, dogs
FAMILY	Canidae	Dogs, foxes, bush dogs, maned wolves
GENUS	Canis	True dogs, such as wolves, coyotes, jackals, domestic dogs
SPECIES	familiaris	Domestic dogs

STORING YOUR COLLECTION

The more you learn about your collection and the larger it grows, the more you'll need to keep it organized. A well-kept collection is like a library: you know how to find the specimens you already have and you have a place to add new ones. You may not want to display all the shells, rocks, and fossils you collect. Here are some ways to store them:

- Shells and many minerals will fade if exposed to direct sunlight over time. Store them away from direct sunlight.

- Fossils and shells that are very delicate or fragile should be stored separately in plastic or cardboard boxes. Most other shells and rocks can be kept in small re-closable plastic bags.

- Cardboard or plastic shoe boxes work very well for storing your bagged specimens: they don't take up a lot of space, and they stack nicely. Clear plastic boxes are ideal because the lids are sturdy, they're water-proof, and you can see what is inside. Labeling the boxes will keep your collection organized and make it easy to find what you're looking for.

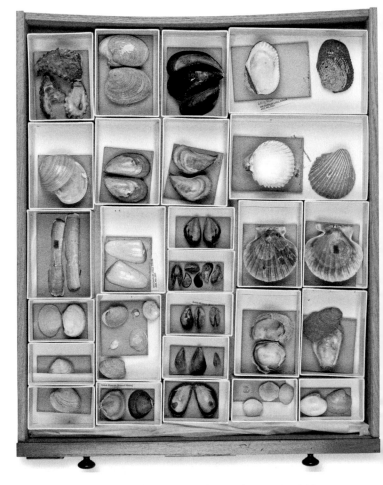

These shells were collected by the great nineteenth-century British naturalist Charles Darwin during his voyages on the HMS *Beagle* between 1831 and 1836. They're now part of the collection of the Natural History Museum in London. Take a tip from the museum curators and use the small boxes that come with jewelry to hold your collection in a drawer. Each little box, padded with cotton, makes the perfect container for a shell, stone, or fossil. Be sure to mark each box with the date you found your specimen, where you found it, and how you've identified it. Mollusk specimen drawer / Natural History Museum, London, UK / Bridgeman Images NHM1458292

CATALOGING YOUR COLLECTION

NUMBERING

Many collectors write a catalog number directly on each specimen so that it can't get mixed up with any others. Start with number 1 and go from there. Then, when you store your shell, rock, or fossil in a box, write the specimen number on the outside lid or side of the box.

Here are three ways to write numbers on a specimen:

1. Make paper dots with a hole punch and write a number on a dot. Use white glue to stick it to the shell, rock, or fossil. White glue will not damage surfaces and, if you need to, you can soak a shell or rock in water to remove the dot and glue.

2. For a light-colored shell or rock with a smooth surface, you can write the number (small!) directly on the surface with a fine pen and India ink. Choose a place where the number will not be obvious.

3. On a dark-colored shell or rock, use white nail polish to paint a small spot on it. Allow the nail polish to dry completely. Carefully write the number on the spot in pen.

Once you've assigned a number to a specimen in your collection, record it in your notebook. Keep a list, starting with number 1, and include the name or a brief description of the specimen. This will become your collection catalog. You'll always be able to find what you're looking for and see how your collection has grown.

This ten-line chafer beetle has been tagged with its name, the date it was found, and its location.

TAGGING

For items in your collection that are too small or too delicate to be numbered directly on the surface, make a tag. Keep the tag with the specimen in a small box or baggie. You can make the tags yourself or buy them. The information that you write on the tag might include the following:

- catalog number

- scientific name

- who collected the specimen

- where it was collected

- when it was collected

- notes with other important information, such as weather conditions or tides

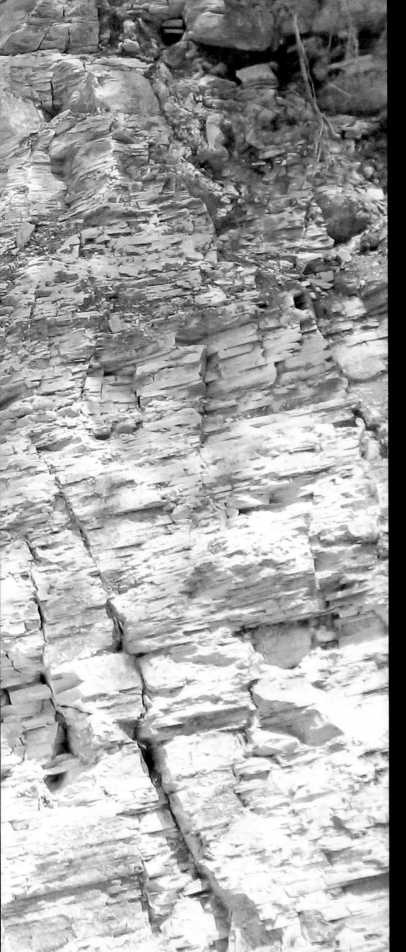

COLLECTING ROCKS AND MINERALS

WHAT ARE ROCKS AND WHAT ARE MINERALS?

Rocks are made from mixtures of two or more kinds of minerals. Of the thousands of minerals known, only about fifty occur frequently in rocks.

Minerals are created naturally from elements in the Earth. The two most common elements are oxygen and silicon and nearly all minerals contain these two. As minerals are created, their molecules stack in a regular pattern, which, if they have room, grow into crystals.

That might make it sound as though all minerals are similar—but they're not! The mineral limonite often has an earthy appearance, galena and pyrite can look like metal, and diamond and quartz crystals are frequently glassy.

About 130 minerals with particularly beautiful color and clarity are valued as gems, but gems vary widely, too. Opal, which is a variety of quartz, often shimmers with colors like sunsets or rainbows. Diamonds, the hardest minerals of all, are formed from carbon, and, if pure, have no color at all.

When the element silicon joins with other elements that give it color, it produces mineral gems such as emerald, topaz, and garnet. The hardest, rarest, and most beautiful minerals—like rubies, emeralds, and diamonds—are known as "precious" gems. Others, like citrines, amethysts, and opals, which are not as rare, are called "semiprecious stones."

Rocks are mixtures of minerals. For instance, granite is made of the minerals quartz, feldspar, and mica, all mixed together. So, rocks differ from one another in weight, color, and shine, depending on the minerals in their composition. But they also differ depending on the way they were formed. There are three types of rocks: igneous, sedimentary, and metamorphic. All three types tell a story about the time and environment when they were formed. As you become familiar with different types of rocks, you will be able to spot which is which quickly and understand the stories that they have to tell.

All of the specimens at right are minerals.

FELDSPAR MICA QUARTZ

OPAL GARNET DIAMOND

EMERALD FLUORITE NICKEL SULFATE

Lava flow in Hawaii

Layers in sedimentary rock

IGNEOUS ROCKS

The *ig* in *igneous* (just as in the word *ignite*) means "fire." Igneous rocks were once molten and are formed from cooled magma and lava. If magma never makes it to the surface in a volcanic eruption, it cools into "plutonic" (underground) igneous rock. The slower the cooling, the larger the crystals. Granite is one type of plutonic igneous rock.

Lava is magma that comes to the surface in a volcanic eruption. Lava cools on the surface of the Earth and produces "volcanic" igneous rocks. Basalt, rhyolite, pumice, and obsidian are volcanic igneous rocks. Obsidian—volcanic glass—is formed from lava that cooled so quickly there wasn't time to form crystals. The people of traditional cultures chipped obsidian to make extremely sharp spear- and arrowheads. If you've ever cut yourself on a piece of glass, you know how sharp the points can be.

SEDIMENTARY ROCKS

Sedimentary rocks are formed from sediment—the pebbles, sand, clay, and silt that are left behind when other rocks are ground down by erosion. Over thousands of years, when the various sediments have been redeposited, mixed, and compacted, they again become a rock. Some common types of sedimentary rocks are sandstone, shale, siltstone, and limestone.

Fossils are most often found embedded in sedimentary rock. (See chapter 4, "Collecting Fossils," page 63.) In fact, limestone is made up from the remains of shells or the skeletons of marine plants and animals mixed with sediment from rocks. In limestone caves, you can often see the shapes of shells and corals in the rock walls. You just might be amazed to discover that inland seas once existed in areas that are now nowhere near the ocean.

Sedimentary rock can range from hard to soft. Limestone is hard enough to be used for constructing buildings, but shale, which is formed from mud or clay, can be soft enough to break into pieces by hand.

METAMORPHIC ROCK

Metamorphosis means "change," and metamorphic rock is any kind of rock that has been changed by intense heat and pressure. Most metamorphic rocks begin deep in the Earth and are pushed to the surface through movements of the Earth's crust when mountains and canyons are formed. Some examples of metamorphic rocks are quartzite, marble, slate, and greenstone.

Quartzite, which is one of the most abundant metamorphic rocks on the Earth's surface, is formed when heat and pressure are applied to sandstone. Similarly, with enough heat and pressure, limestone becomes marble, shale becomes slate, basalt becomes greenstone, and granite becomes gneiss (pronounced "nice").

GRANITE (igneous)

BASALT (igneous)

OBSIDIAN (igneous)

RHYOLITE (igneous)

SANDSTONE (sedimentary)

SHALE (sedimentary)

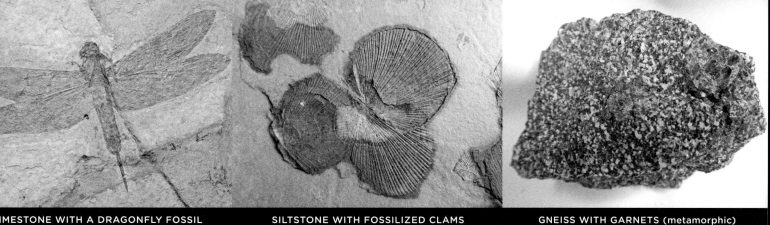

IMESTONE WITH A DRAGONFLY FOSSIL
(sedimentary)

SILTSTONE WITH FOSSILIZED CLAMS
(sedimentary)

GNEISS WITH GARNETS (metamorphic)

LAPIS LAZULI (metamorphic)

PYRITE CRYSTALS IN QUARTZITE (metamorphic)

NEPHRITE (metamorphic)

WHERE TO LOOK AND WHAT TO COLLECT

You might become intrigued with rocks when you're walking on a beach, hiking in the mountains, exploring a cave, or digging a garden in your own backyard. The kinds of rocks you find are different in the mountains than they are on flat prairie land. They are different along the shorelines than they are in the middle of the country—all depending on the effects of glaciers, wind, rain, or volcanoes as the landscape is transformed.

To help you decide where to look and what to collect, start by doing a little research on the geology in your corner of the world. Learn how the land and rocks were formed where you are. There are many books that can help you learn where to look and what to expect to find (see the book list on page 122). Go online and find pictures and information on your local rocks or visit a natural history museum near you, and then start hunting!

Once you start venturing out of your own backyard to look for rocks and minerals, check before you collect! Mineral rights are owned by whoever owns the property they are on. Before setting out, make sure you identify areas where collecting is allowed or get permission from private property owners. Joining a rock and mineral collecting club is a great way to learn from others and gain access to caves and mines or to mineral-rich areas.

SUPPLIES

If you are a serious rock and mineral collector, you'll need certain supplies when you plan your collecting trip:

- A backpack will make it much easier to carry any specimens you find.

- Newspaper, re-closable plastic bags, cotton balls, and empty pill bottles. Rocks can be more delicate than you think! Wrapping bulky rocks in newspaper protects both them and your pack from damage. Wrapping tiny fragments in cotton balls and placing them in pill bottles will keep them safe.

- If you are collecting in an area where the rocks cannot be picked up loose, you'll need a rock hammer, eye protection, and gloves.

- A notebook. Have your journal or another notebook handy when you are out in the field.

Young geologist with a rock hammer

INFORMATION TO INCLUDE IN YOUR JOURNAL

- Where you found your rock or mineral specimen.

- Whether it was loose or part of a larger rock. What other kinds of rocks were nearby?

- How or why you noticed it.

- A rough sketch or photo of the location and the specimen on-site.

- What kind of rock you thought it was when you spotted it and why. Compare those notes with what you learn after you bring the rock home and do some research.

- A story about what happened while you were collecting. Funny or interesting stories help you remember your trip.

HOW TO CLEAN AND CARE FOR YOUR COLLECTION

A good cleaning can reveal the true beauty of your specimen.

Most rocks and minerals can be rinsed in warm water. Use old toothbrushes, dish brushes, and small paintbrushes to clean tight spaces. Adding some dish soap to the water will help loosen stubborn dirt.

Some minerals, such as halite (rock salt), sylvite (potassium chloride), and borax, will dissolve in water. You can clean them with a cotton swab or paper towel soaked in rubbing alcohol. Wear gloves while using any cleaners: alcohol will dry out your skin.

A dental pick is a good tool for scraping off crusts that have accumulated on rock or mineral surfaces and for digging dirt out of cracks and holes.

A rock tumbler and rocks polished with different grits

ADD A LITTLE POLISH

Many of the harder rocks and minerals can be polished using a rock tumbler. If you use a tumbler, here are some important things to keep in mind:

- Always follow the manufacturer's directions, and change grits and water as instructed.

- Always put similar-size rocks in the tumbler. Smaller than average specimens will be ground away to nothing if they're paired with large rocks!

- Only combine rocks or minerals of similar hardness in the tumbler.

- Be patient. It takes a while for tumbled rocks to reach a nice polish.

Sometimes you'll have happy surprises with rock tumbling. Jim, a rock and mineral polishing studio master, had some minerals he wanted to polish in his rock tumbler. He didn't have enough specimens to fill the tub, so he added some ordinary landscape rocks just to bring it to the right level. When the polishing was done, one chunk of landscape rock turned out to be his most beautiful piece: it was a pink moonstone!

ADD SOME GLOSS

Adding a light coat of silicone spray, mineral oil, cedarwood oil, or balsam oil will hide fine scratches that make a rock look dull. Some minerals, including thenardite, borax, hanksite, and blödite, have water in their structure and will become dry and crumbly if not coated with a light coat of oil.

With time, oil coatings will rub off or will be absorbed by the rock, making it look dull again. Be careful to clean off any leftover oils before you add more.

Project: Make a Display Board

To display your collection of rocks or fossils you'll need a frame with a sturdy backing. This simple display board is made of plywood and pine molding. We've left our board plain, but you can paint or varnish yours if you like. Make sure the varnish or paint is completely dry before gluing in your rock specimens or hanging the display board on the wall!

1. Set the piece of plywood on your work surface. Line up a piece of molding along one edge of the plywood. Line up a second piece of molding perpendicular to the first, along the next edge. Press the two pieces together and mark the first piece at the edge of the plywood.

2. Cut the molding at the marked spot with a thin-blade saw. (A miter box helps you make straight cuts.) If you are using $\frac{1}{2}$" (1.3 cm) molding, the piece should be $11\frac{1}{2}$" (29.2 cm) long.

YOU WILL NEED:

- 12" x 12" (30.5 x 30.5 cm) sheet of $\frac{1}{4}$" (6 mm) plywood

- two $3\frac{1}{2}$' (107 cm) lengths of $\frac{1}{2}$" (1.3 cm) molding

- pencil

- thin-blade saw

- miter box (optional)

- ruler

- craft glue

- wax paper

- books or other heavy objects

- picture hanger and nails

- hammer

3

4

3. Use the first piece of wood as a measure for three more. Cut the pieces with the saw. You now have a plywood back, and four sections for the frame. Line up the frame on the plywood to make sure everything fits correctly.

4. To make dividers, measure and cut one 11" (28 cm) piece of molding and two 5¼" (13.3 cm) sections.

5. Now you're ready to glue. Apply glue to one 11½" (29.2 cm) piece of the frame and press it firmly onto the plywood. Do the same with the other frame sections.

5

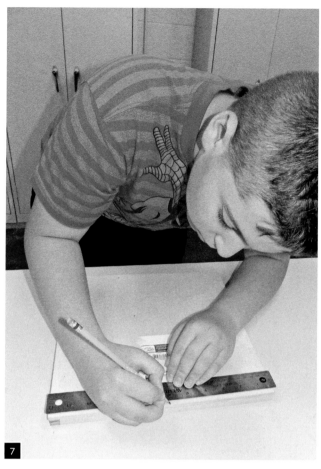

6. Next, glue in the dividers, being careful to keep the frame in place. Let the glue set up for at least a couple of hours before going on to the next step. If the wood begins to curl as the glue dries, cover it with a sheet or two of wax paper and place some books on top.

7. When the glue is completely dry, turn the display board over. Measure and mark the center of one edge.

8. Center the hanger and nail it into place.

9

9. You have a display board! Attach light rocks or fossils with hot glue.

10. Use this as a guide; be creative and try different thicknesses of wood for your frame. You can add in or leave out dividers, too!

INTERVIEW: A Budding Scientist

Anna, with part of her collection

Anna is not sure why she likes geology so much. "It's come easy to me and it fascinates me no matter how deep I go into the subject," she says. "I love that I can look at different geologic structures—like mountains and mesas and volcanic plains—and tell you how they were formed, what rocks they are composed of, and all kinds of other things." For that matter, she explains, she can "pick up any rock—anywhere—and know how it was formed."

She also loves "finding new and interesting samples, learning about them, and sharing what I've learned with other people." But her passion does have its consequences. "Sometimes I'll be walking along with someone having a pleasant conversation, when all of a sudden I see an interesting rock. I act like a dog does with a squirrel—completely leaving the conversation behind to look at the rock! This has happened way too often!"

Although she'd have a hard time naming a favorite rock or mineral, Anna says her specimen of vanadinite is definitely toward the top of her list. But, she continues, "I

At age twelve, Anna started collecting rocks and minerals when she participated in a national science competition called the Science Olympiad. The Olympiad has many categories for competition, including sections on rocks and minerals, fossils, engineering, and bridge building.

"The funny thing is," Anna says, "originally, I really didn't want to be put in the rocks and minerals event, but, by the end of the following year, I was completely obsessed!" From then on, her collection has grown. "I wanted to collect *everything*. Now I have over a hundred different specimens and counting!"

Anna keeps her smallest rock samples protected in plastic storage boxes.

Anna's beautiful vanadinite specimen is among her favorites.

like my chalcedony geode, my basalt-and-olivine specimen, a 3-inch (7.5 cm) ammonite that is still in the rock, a garnet-mica schist, my labradorite, and every fossil I have ever collected and . . . okay, I'll stop there . . . "

When she first started collecting, Anna kept her specimens in clear compartmented storage boxes. Soon she was moving to larger and larger containers and started displaying especially nice-looking pieces on shelves where she could enjoy them. They are now on display all around her room. But she still keeps her smallest specimens in compartmented boxes.

What started as a hobby has become something she may someday want to do for a living. "Studying rocks and minerals has made me realize my love for it—and how little most people know about geology. Whatever I end up doing, I'm sure rocks will be a part of it." In the meantime, Anna says that she is "excitedly waiting for the time when I'm flying somewhere and someone who helps me with my bag asks, 'Gee, what do you have in here . . . rocks?' and I can honestly reply, 'As a matter of fact, yes!'"

A Collector of Memories

Some of us just love our collections because they remind us of travels, friends, family, and special times in nature.

Mikayla, who lives far from the sea, was six years old when she collected tiny seashells on a beach in Texas. Mikayla's next trip to a coast was when she and her family went to Oregon. This time, she was eleven. Her collection of tiny seashells grew—each one reminding her of her shoreline visits and her love for the sea.

When she's out hiking, Mikayla also likes to collect heart-shaped rocks. She showed me one that was barely an inch (2.5 cm) long, and then dragged out one that weighs 25 pounds (11.3 kg). "I found this one when we went to Oregon," she says. "I stuck it in the trunk of our car, and Dad found it when we got home!"

Mikayla's fossil-hunting forays also connect with many memories. Recalling her first fossil-hunting trip with some friends, she says, "I found a complete fish fossil—then accidentally dropped it in the river! I was so disappointed!" But she found other small fossils and took them home as reminders of her trip.

When she was in the fifth grade, she placed many of her treasures in a "memory box." "I always look through all the treasures I've saved when I add another item," she says. They're all reminders of her best experiences (so far).

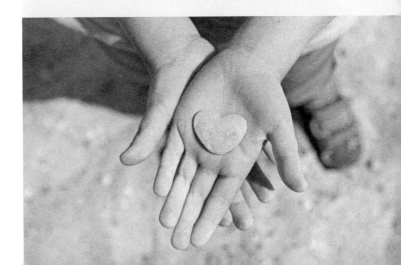

GEODES AND CRYSTALS: WHY SOME ROCKS GET ALL THE BLING

Geodes begin as a cavity, or hollow space, in a rock. A cavity can be produced any number of ways, including, for example, gas bubbles in cooled magma, or the hollow space between the two halves of a fossilized clam shell embedded in rock.

Although rocks look solid, there are often cracks and pores through which water can move. As water slowly flows through a rock, it dissolves minerals. When the mineral-rich water reaches the empty space in the rock, the minerals separate out of the watery solution and begin to form crystals on the inside of the cavity. Geodes grow from the outside in, so the outermost layer, that actually touches the rock, is the oldest.

There are a number of reasons why geodes are hollow. In some, the supply of mineral-rich water may be cut off. In others, the geode may erode out of the parent rock, or the growing crystals block the holes and cracks in the rock, preventing the seepage of any more water.

An amethyst geode and a blue agate geode

Geodes are often filled with quartz; if the quartz is purple, it is called amethyst. Some geodes and agates, such as this blue agate specimen, are artificially dyed to give them their bright color.

ABOVE: A collection of uncut geodes.

RIGHT: A geode sliced in half with a special saw.

An opal geode formed when water seeped into this ammonite fossil.

Geodes are found all over the world—from Iceland and Siberia, to Australia and Brazil—most commonly in places that have seen a lot of volcanic activity, or places with limestone deposits. In the United States, there are geode beds in Southern California, Arizona, New Mexico, Texas, Nevada, Utah, Oregon, Indiana, Kentucky, Ohio, Missouri, and New Jersey. And Iowa's state rock is the geode.

One of the best ways to find geodes is to connect with a gem and mineral club in your area. Such clubs often have access to places you can't normally go, and they can help you "get your eyes on" to see what you are looking for in the field.

Every one is different! An azurite geode and striped agate geode.

Project: **Grow Your Own Crystals**

YOU WILL NEED:

- measuring cup

- 1 cup (235 ml) hot tap water

- clean pint (500 ml) jar

- 1 cup (244 g) Epsom salt

- disposable spoon

- string

- pencil or craft stick

- large paper clip

EPSOM SALT CRYSTALS

You can grow your own crystals quickly by using Epsom salt, a mineral deposit (magnesium sulfate) also called *epsomite*. Epsom salt is most often used for household cleaning and can be found where laundry products are sold.

1. Pour the hot water from the tap into the jar. Don't use boiling water—it could cause problems for growing the crystals.

2. Add the Epsom salt to the water a spoonful at a time. Stir until it has dissolved. Keep adding spoonfuls of Epsom salt until the water is fully saturated. This can take a couple of minutes, depending on the water temperature. You'll know it's fully saturated when some Epsom salt remains on the bottom of the jar no matter how much you stir.

3. Tie one end of the string to the middle of a pencil or craft stick. Tie the other end of the string to the paper clip. The string should be just long enough to reach the bottom of the jar. Drop the paper clip into the jar. Place the pencil or craft stick across the mouth of the jar.

TABLE SALT CRYSTALS

This crystal-growing method is slow, but it's interesting to watch over time.

YOU WILL NEED:

- 3 pint (500 ml) jars
- water
- teaspoon
- table salt
- string
- pencil
- scissors
- paper towel

1. Fill one pint jar with room-temperature water. Add a teaspoon of salt and stir until it dissolves. Keep adding salt by the spoonful, and stirring until no more will dissolve. You will see that some salt crystals have settled to the bottom of the jar. You now have a saturated solution.

2. Pour the saturated solution into another pint jar so that it is about two-thirds full. *Make sure that none of the undissolved salt on the bottom of first jar pours into the second jar.*

3. Tie the string to a pencil. Cut the string so it does not touch the bottom of the jar.

4. Lower the string into the jar of solution.

5. Place a small piece of paper towel over the mouth of the jar to keep out dust but still allow evaporation.

6. Pour the remainder of the solution into the other pint jar (it's okay to have some undissolved salt in this one). Screw on the lid to prevent evaporation.

7. Start looking for crystals to form on the string in the first jar. This might take several days because the growth depends on evaporation, rather than cooling, of the water.

8. For larger crystals, as water evaporates from jar 1, replace it with more saturated solution from jar 2.

9. When you are happy with your crystals, pull up the string and allow the crystals to dry.

4. Put the container in the refrigerator. Crystals will start to grow fairly quickly, but the longer you leave them, the larger your crystals will grow.

5. When you're happy with your crystals, carefully break the crust that will have formed on the water surface. Pull the string from the solution and allow the crystals to dry. They're ready for display. (If you allow the crystals to sit in room-temperature water, they will lose their needle-like sharpness.)

Note: If you'd like to make colorful crystals, add a few drops of food coloring to the water at the end of step 1.

COLLECTING ANIMAL AND BIRD TRACKS

TRACKING BEHAVIOR

Would you believe that you can collect an animal's behavior? That is exactly what you are doing when you collect animal tracks. There are more animals around us than you might think, but they often come out only at night, are shy, or are good at moving around without being seen. Study the tracks and you'll know what kind of animal passed by. You can find out whether an animal was walking or running, whether it's active during the day or at night, and whether it moves around in groups or is solitary. You can even tell whether the animal is healthy or injured!

Any creature that walks, swims, slithers, or flies can leave a track. The prints made by bugs walking on sand often look like tiny tire tracks. Birds often leave prints of their feet on sand and in mud, and will sometimes leave a print of their wing tips as they take off in flight. If a fish is in shallow enough water, it can leave fin prints in the mud as it makes its way to deeper water.

Some insects, like this Moroccan black beetle, leave prints that look like tire tracks.

CAT	FOX	STRIPED SKUNK
BOBCAT	FISHER	MOUSE
OTTER	DOG	MINK
WEASEL	RACCOON	COYOTE
PORCUPINE	BEAVER	BLACK BEAR
OPOSSUM	LYNX	MUSKRAT
BADGER	RABBIT	GRAY SQUIRREL
WOLF	MOOSE	WHITETAIL DEER
ELK/RED DEER	CROW	TURKEY
RUFFED GROUSE	MOUNTAIN LION	DUCK

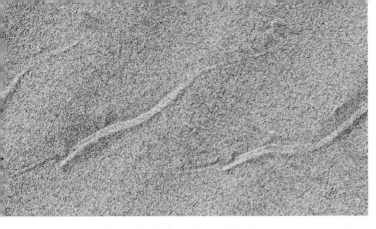

Not all tracks are left by feet. A snake left these tracks in the sand.

By looking at prehistoric animal tracks and burrows, paleontologists have been able to figure out how fast dinosaurs moved. The fastest speed calculated from a medium-size dinosaur trackway was about 27 miles per hour. Another trackway site shows herding behavior: the footprints are of different-size animals, all of the same species, moving in the same direction.

Several different types of dinosaurs left these fossilized tracks in Colorado.

WHERE TO LOOK

Look for tracks in areas where the soil is soft and has just enough "give" to create a good impression. Moist soil, muddy stream banks, beaches, sand dunes after a storm, and freshly fallen snow are all great places to look for tracks. Places where two habitats meet, such as a meadow and a forest, or where a river runs through desert, are especially good for tracks because these areas are apt to have a larger variety of animals.

Bird tracks in fresh snow

KEEPING RECORDS IN YOUR NOTEBOOK

Keep records with photographs and drawings when you find tracks. This information will help you understand what the animal was doing while it was leaving its prints.

1. Where did you find the track? This can provide a clue as to what type of animal left it. The tracks of beavers, muskrats, or turtles, for instance, are most likely to be found close to water where they live. The tracks of animals, such as bobcats, coyotes, or bears, might only show up near water when the animal goes there for a drink.

   For a real-world example, deer tracks were found in and around a cemetery. What were the deer doing there? The landscape around the cemetery was high and dry desert grassland, with very little to eat in winter. However, people left fresh flowers there, especially on weekends. Deer visited the cemetery on weekend nights, nibbling on the fresh greens! If records were not kept, this pattern would have been lost.

2. When were the tracks made? Another example of why it's a good idea to keep records is because some animals only come out after a seasonal event, such as the spring thaw or after a heavy rain.

   An incredible sight in many deserts of the American Southwest is the emergence of spadefoot toads, which come out of a deep sleep after heavy thundershowers. The storms flood and fill temporary ponds, and within hours there may be thousands of little

The tracks in this soft sand near water include black bear, raccoon, ground squirrel, and coyote.

toads hopping around a pond, eating and mating as quickly as they can. In an amazing display of timing, sometimes after only one night of activity, they will burrow back into the mud, waiting for the next thunderstorm to wake them up. The next morning there will be hundreds of tiny toad footprints in the mud around the pond. But mixed with the toad prints are tracks left by thirsty animals drawn to the water, and by predators that came looking for something to eat.

COLLECTING TRACKS WITH A CAMERA

One advantage to taking photographs is that it allows you to collect a lot more information than you can by simply making a cast of a print—but only if you are a careful photographer!

Along with photographing a close-up of a print, step back and photograph the trackway. This will provide clues as to where the animal was coming from and where it was going. It can also indicate whether the animal was alone and how quickly it was moving.

TIPS FOR PHOTOGRAPHING TRACKS

1. Show the size. Include a ruler in the photograph if you have one. No ruler? Use a pencil, a coin, or your hand or foot.

Here's one way to measure the size of a dinosaur track!

2. Take photos in the morning or late afternoon. Many prints will be much easier to see during the early morning or late afternoon hours when shadows are long. The shadows can help define a print's shape in a photograph.

3. Take the picture from directly above the print—but try to keep your own shadow out of the way! Taking a photo from an angle can make it difficult to see the details.

4. Take a photo of the trail left by the animal. You can learn whether the animal was alone or in a group, and whether it was walking, running, or hopping.

When you've printed a photograph of a track or trackway, keep it in an album or your journal. Include any information you may have collected, such as what animal made the track, the date, and time of day.

These raccoon prints, made in the mud, were photographed from directly above the prints.

Stepping back to photograph tracks will let you see where the animal was going.

Project: Making Casts of Tracks

YOU WILL NEED:

- cardboard milk carton

- scissors

- paper clips

- container for mixing the plaster (a large plastic cup or plastic bag will work)

- water

- plaster of Paris (available at any hardware store)

- mixing stick

- pencil

You can make plaster casts of animal and bird tracks in the soil and even in the snow! The two procedures are very similar, but working in snow takes a little more patience.

CASTS IN SOIL

1. Choose an animal track that's deep enough to show good detail. Clear away loose leaves, sticks, and rocks that could become stuck in your cast.

2. Cut the milk carton into strips with scissors. Sections should be about 2½" (6.5 cm) wide by 12" to 15" (30.5–38 cm) long. Bend the strips to form a ring that will be large enough to fit around the animal track with a 1" (2.5 cm) margin all around. Use paper clips to hold the ring together. The ring will contain the plaster. The wax coating on the strips will prevent the cardboard from sticking to the plaster.

3. Press the ring into the soil, making sure that at least 1" (2.5 cm) remains above ground.

4. Now it is time to mix the plaster of Paris. Set out the mixing container. Pour in about half as much water as you think will fill the ring.

5. Add twice as much plaster as you have water. For example, if you start with 1 cup of water, you will need to add 2 cups of plaster.

6. Mix the plaster well with the stick. If you are using a bag, squeeze the contents of the bag to mix well. You want the mix to have the same texture as pancake batter.

7

8

7. Carefully pour the plaster over the track. If you are working on a very large track, fill the track first, then fill in the remainder of the ring. For smaller tracks, pour the plaster next to the track, and allow it to flow in, filling the track. Then finish filling the ring.

8. If you want to hang your print when it is done, make a hanger that will set into the cast. Open out a paper clip and bend it into a U-shape. Insert the open end of the paper clip into the plaster so that the U-shaped loop remains exposed.

9. Allow the plaster to set. This can take some time, depending on the temperature. Wait at least 20 to 25 minutes, then test to see whether the plaster has set by touching it. If it feels solid, you can start to remove it from the soil.

9

10. Carefully dig out the cardboard ring and lift it, plaster, soil, and all. Remove the paper clips and the cardboard, and brush away some of the dirt.

11. Wait at least 24 hours before trying to wash and clean the cast—if you try any earlier, it could crumble and fall apart!

12. Use the pencil to write the date and where the print came from on the cast.

CASTS IN SNOW

This is a variation on the previous mold-making project. To make the snow print sturdy enough to hold the plaster, you will spritz it with ice water and let the water freeze. This will give the print a firm base—but you have to be patient while it freezes.

YOU WILL NEED:

- spray bottle
- ice water
- cardboard milk carton
- scissors
- paper clips
- container for mixing the plaster
- plaster of Paris (available at any hardware store)
- mixing stick

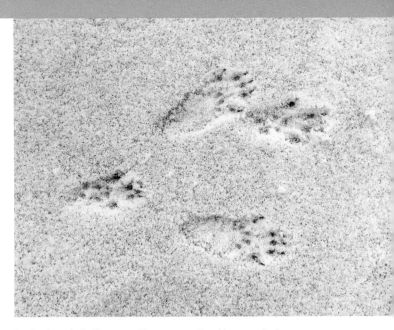

Squirrel tracks in the snow. The process of making a cast of an animal track in the snow requires a thin coating of ice in the track.

1. Fill the spray bottle with ice-cold water. You might want to mix snow into the water to cool it even more. Colder is better!

2. Locate an animal footprint with good depth and detail. Lightly mist the print with water. This will freeze and make a thin layer of ice on the inside of the print.

3. Cut the milk carton into strips with scissors. Sections should be about 2½" (6.5 cm) wide by 12" to 15" (30.5–38 cm) long. Bend the strips to form a ring that will be large enough to fit around the animal track with a 1" (2.5 cm) margin all around. Use paper clips to hold the ring together. The ring will contain the plaster. The wax coating on the strips will prevent the cardboard from sticking to the plaster.

4. Press the ring into the snow, making sure that at least 1" (2.5 cm) remains above ground.

5. Set out the container for mixing the plaster. Using ice water, pour in about half as much water as you think will fill the ring.

6. Add twice as much plaster as you have water. For example, if you start with 1 cup of water, you will need to add 2 cups of plaster.

7. Mix the plaster well with the stick. It should have the same texture as pancake batter.

8. Carefully pour the plaster over the track. If you are working on a very large track, fill the track first, then fill in the remainder of the ring. For smaller tracks, pour the plaster next to the track, and allow it to flow in, filling the track. Then finish filling the ring.

9. If you want to hang your print when it is done, make a hanger that will set into the cast. Open out a paper clip and bend it into a U-shape. Insert the open end of the paper clip into the plaster so that the U-shaped loop remains exposed.

10. Now you have to wait! Because the snow is so cold, the plaster might take as long as a day to set. When the plaster has set, carefully remove it from the snow, bring it indoors, and allow it to dry for at least 24 hours.

MAKE A TRACK RECORDING STATION

If you do a lot of camping or you live near a wilderness area where you frequently come across animal tracks, make a track recording station. This will allow you to keep a record of all the animals that might walk through a particular place.

Select a path or another area where you have seen animal tracks before. Many animals use the same trails over and over again. This is a perfect place to set up. The area should be free from any plants. Under best conditions, a 6' (183 cm) wide path is ideal.

Use a heavy rake to clear away sticks, stones, or leaves that might interfere with an animal leaving tracks. Then use a garden rake to loosen the soil, making it fluffy and level. Your "recording station" is now set and all you have to do is wait.

Inspect your station the next day. Any animals that might have walked through your area will have left clear tracks on the surface you prepared. You can now photograph or make casts of the prints you captured.

Select a path where you've seen animal tracks before. Clear it with a rake, then all you have to do is wait!

DISPLAYING YOUR COLLECTION OF TRACKS

There are many ways to organize your collection. If you're keeping a scrapbook or album, organize the photos by family. Have a section of your album for carnivores, another section for deer, or a section for mice or invertebrates.

Arrange your photos, drawings, or molds of tracks by where they came from. This is interesting because it gives you an idea of which animals might interact with each other, and who shares your neighborhood.

Organize by size. If you keep plaster casts of prints, arrange them on a shelf by size—one shelf for all the small ones, another for medium-size tracks, and another for the really big ones.

Share your knowledge. Do you know what kind of creature left this track that looks like a toothy smile? It was a magpie, taking flight. The "smile" is the spread of its tail feathers.

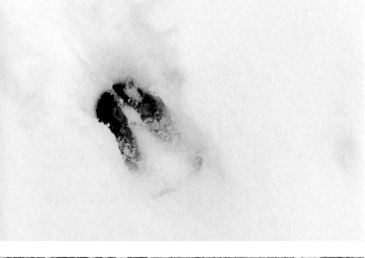

Contribute to Science

If you enjoy collecting tracks, you might want to download iNaturalist (inaturalist.org) to your phone. iNaturalist is a citizen science project and network of naturalists, scientists, biologists, and interested people where they can share notes on biology from around the world. The section on tracking can be found at www.inaturalist .org/projects/north-american-animal-tracking -database. By contributing, you add to the body of scientific knowledge.

Grouping your photos can help you study details. Here is a deer leaving tracks—and close-ups of its tracks in snow and mud.

COLLECTING
SEASHELLS

MEET THE MOLLUSKS

Shells are produced by mollusks, a group of animals that includes snails, clams, and octopuses. The mollusk family is enormous and the varieties of these animals have distinct shells—many of them very beautiful— which make them fun and fascinating to collect.

TWO FAMILIAR TYPES

The two main types of shells you're apt to come across on a beach come from *bivalves* and *gastropods*.

A complete bivalve shell has two similar parts called valves (*bi* means "two") that are connected along one edge with a rubbery ligament that allows the two parts to open like a hinge. These include clams, scallops, mussels, cockles, oysters, jingle shells, and many more. You're most likely to find only half of a bivalve lying on the beach, but if you're lucky you might find one with the two valves still hinged together and the animal that once lived inside it gone.

Snail, or gastropod, shells protect animals that travel on their stomachs (*gastropod* means "stomach-foot"). These include abalones, whelks, conches, periwinkles, turbos, cowries, slipper shells, and others—lots of others.

A bivalve hinge allows the two halves of the shell (in this case, a cockle shell) to open and close when the animal inside needs to eat, move, or hide. You won't often find both halves connected, because the hinge easily breaks apart once the animal dies. The colored stripes on each half show how the shell grew when the animal inside was alive.

Gastropods usually have a single shell (univalve). Most, but not all, are formed as a spiral. Around the world, you'll find gastropod shells in an amazing array of colors and colored patterns that allow the living animal to camouflage itself in its surroundings or ward off predators. From top to bottom, left to right, the gastropods here include cerith, conch, whelk, cowrie, cone, and spiny murex shells.

HOW TO BUILD YOUR COLLECTION

Water temperature and the type of foods available in the ocean are two of the many things that determine what kinds of shellfish thrive in each part of the world. So, if you visit the same shoreline often, or if you are collecting close to home, you'll start seeing the same kinds of shells over and over. If you travel to another place, or maybe even a rocky area of the same beach, you will likely find completely different shells. Visiting as many different *habitats* as you can is one of the best ways to grow your collection.

1. Did you find several different types of shells on the beach and wonder what they're called?

   After bringing home your finds, there are many ways to identify your shells. Some books that can help you are listed in the resource section on page 122. As your interest and your collection grow, so will the list of books you should consider adding to your library. You can also do an online search for the kinds of seashells in your region. Make a list or print one out to keep in your field journal. Compare your shells with the ones on the list. It can be very rewarding to find a new shell and to be able to check it off. You'll soon develop a "collector's eye," spotting the best examples of each. Make a point of reading about the shellfish in your region: where they live, what they eat, and how they grow.

2. Was it a particular type of shell that caught your attention first?

   Let's say you found a pretty, fan-shaped scallop shell. If you look for others, you'll discover that scallop shells range in color from white to blue-gray to orange and brown. Some might have arched stripes like a rainbow. Some have speckled colors. You'll also discover that you can find scallop shells in many sizes. If those things intrigue you, then let color and size guide your collecting habits. Read about how scallops grow their shells, and what scallops in other parts of the world look like.

   If your family is traveling to a beach somewhere in the world, do a little research before you go. Find out what kinds of shells you're apt to find. Print out pictures of the shells and their names, and note which ones are common and which are rare. You'll be prepared to build on your collection as soon as you get to the beach and will bring your expertise with you. Be sure to rinse those new shells before you put them in your suitcase!

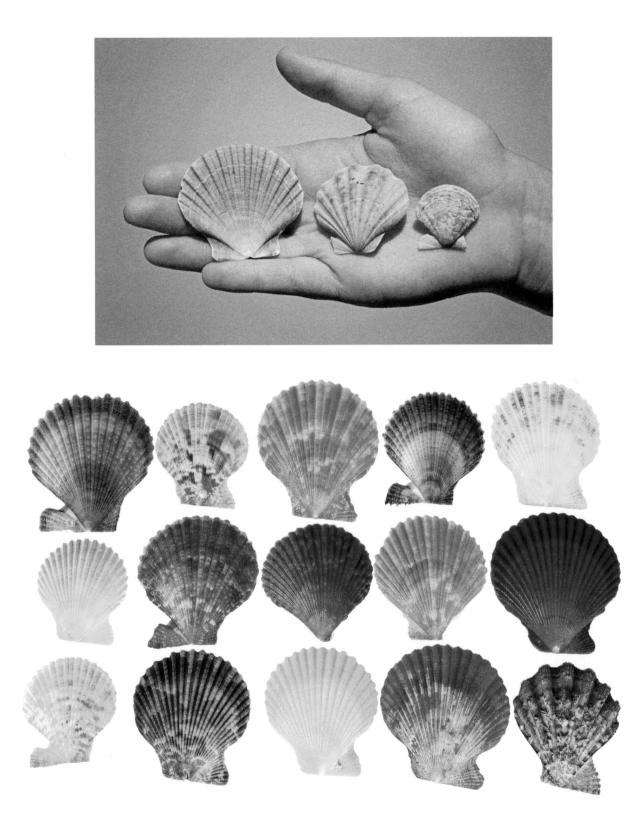

Some collectors like to focus on a single type of shell and collect it in all its variety. You can collect scallops, for instance, by their size or by their color. And, if you travel, you'll find different types of scallops in different parts of the world.

Be a Savvy Collector

There are good times to collect shells—and then there are great times!

- **After a storm:** Seashells wash up on beaches after a storm. Look in tidal pools and between rocks. You'll also find shells by gently pulling apart clumps of seaweed.

- **Low tides:** Low tides happen twice a day, and on a new or full moon tides are extra low and more sand is exposed. Those are the times you can collect shells that don't often show up on the beach.

- **Morning:** Be an early bird. Shells wash onto shore at night and, if you are out before anyone else, you are more likely to find the best.

Be a Conscientious Collector

- Collect only dead shells; make sure there is no animal living in a shell that you pick up. Keep your eyes open for hermit crabs: remember that animals other than the one that made the shell might be using it for a home.

- Take only as many shells as you need for your collection, and perhaps a few more to trade with friends.

- Check to see whether there are any local rules that prohibit collection of shells. In some places, beaches and tidal pools are protected, and visitors are not allowed to keep even dead shells.

Collector's Checklist

☐ Sunscreen, sunglasses, and a hat: shell collecting is fun but a sunburn is not!

☐ Sandals, sneakers, or bare feet? If you are walking on rocks and looking in tidal pools, wear an old pair of sandals or sneakers you don't mind getting wet. Rocks on the shore can be slippery and broken shells can cause cuts, so be careful where you place your feet. On sandy beaches, nothing beats walking barefoot.

☐ A bucket or basket and sandwich bags: a small plastic bucket will make carrying your treasures easier. Sandwich bags help protect fragile specimens.

☐ A small hand rake is useful when looking through seaweed, reaching into cracks in rocks, or digging out partially buried shells from the sand.

☐ A notebook is a good idea if you want to record information about the shells you collect.

CARING FOR YOUR COLLECTION

Remember the word *curator* means "to take care of." Taking care of a shell collection begins with cleaning away the sand, mud, dried seaweed, salt, and barnacles that often cling to surfaces. Here are some methods:

1. **Easy rinse and brush.** Most shells need only a rinse or a soak in cool fresh water and a brushing with an old toothbrush to remove sand and dirt. Adding dish soap to the water will help remove stubborn dirt. Use a garden hose sprayer to rinse the shells inside and out.

2. **Get off the gunk with water and bleach.** Bleach will remove all kinds of stubborn gunk and barnacles from a shell, and, surprisingly, it will not affect the shell's color! However, be careful not to soak very fragile shells—bleach can cause thin shells to become very brittle. *Be sure to have an adult help if you use bleach.* Wear rubber gloves, eye protection, and clothing that you don't mind getting splashed with bleach. **WARNING:** Never mix cleaning chemicals: chlorine plus ammonia gives off toxic gases.

Pull on your gloves and measure an amount of water into a bucket. Carefully add an equal amount of bleach. Slowly (so it won't splash) place the shells in the solution and watch carefully: algae and other things that have grown on the shell will begin to bleach and flake off.

When the bleach is no longer cleaning the shell, take it out, rinse it in fresh water, and then brush it with a stiff brush or toothbrush. When you have removed what you can from the shell, place it in clean water to clean off any remaining chlorine. Be sure to rinse the bucket or bowl carefully, too.

Clean sand, mud, and seaweed from shells with a simple rinse or soak in water.

A soak in a bleach solution loosens barnacles on shells. After the soak, rinse the shell and then use a toothbrush or another stiff brush to get rid of the barnacles.

3. **Boil it.** Sometimes you'll find a shell that has held on to bits of the animal that once lived inside it. These can get very smelly if not properly cleaned. If you can't pick the bits out with tweezers or rinse them out with a jet from a hose, then boil the shell. *Be sure to have an adult help if you use the stove.*

   Put the shells in a saucepan of *cool* water. Place the pan on the stove and slowly bring it to a boil. Avoid putting shells directly into boiling water because that can cause them to crack or cause their surfaces to become permanently cloudy.

   Allow the shells to boil for about a minute per inch (2.5 cm) of length, then turn off the stove. Use a slotted spoon to pull the smallest shell out first. When it's cool enough to touch, use tweezers to remove any remaining animal parts. Move on to the next largest shell.

   Allow the shells to cool slowly: putting hot shells into cold water can also cause them to crack. Use a garden-hose sprayer to flush even the smallest amount of tissue that might be left behind. Allow the shell to dry.

ADD A LITTLE SHINE

Often, a shell will look beautiful when it's wet and in the sun, but dull after it's dried. If you want to restore the shine, wipe the shell with a small amount of mineral oil or a squirt of WD-40 and a soft cloth.

To keep your shells looking great, keep them out of direct sunlight! Brightly colored shells will fade to dull yellow, pink, or white if exposed to the sun over time.

How NOT to Clean a Shell

What you do not want to do is clean your shells with any kind of acid. Even edible acids, like vinegar, will eat away at the surface of a shell, making it bumpy or chalky or, worse, dissolving it completely.

YOU WILL NEED:

- clean corrugated-cardboard pizza box
- ruler
- marker
- scissors
- clear acetate sheet
- packing tape
- construction paper
- glue stick
- glue gun

Making a shadow box is a great way to show off items from your collection, whether they are shells, rocks, fossils, or cones and seeds. The outside of the box forms a frame and window for display, and the inside provides a protective, dust-free case. We've used a stiff cardboard pizza box for our shadow box. Pizza boxes are a good choice because they are shallow, one piece, and available in a variety of sizes.

1. Unfold the edges of the box and lay it flat on your work surface with the printed side up. (The printing will end up on the inside of the shadow box, so it won't show.)

2. Decide how large you want the opening to be. Measure in from each side on the lid of the box and draw lines to show the size and shape of the window.

3. Use scissors to carefully cut out the window.

4. Measure the opening of the window. Cut a piece of acetate that is at least 1" (2.5 cm) wider and 1" (2.5 cm) longer than the opening. Center the acetate over the opening.

5. Apply packing tape around the four edges of the acetate to hold the window in place.

6. Measure the inside flat surface of the shadow box. Cut a piece of construction paper to that size. Glue the construction paper into place with a glue stick.

7. Fold in the edges to reassemble the box and you're ready to go!

💡 VARIATION: Hang it Up

If you want to hang your shadow box on the wall, add a hanger. Before gluing in the construction paper to the inner surface of the shadow box in step 6, carefully use the point of your scissors to make two small holes, about 1½" (3.8 cm) apart, about 1" (2.5 cm) down from the top. Thread a string through the two holes and knot the ends on the outside of the box. Now you can line the box with a piece of colored construction paper and add your treasures.

8

9

8. Open the box. Choose the pieces that you want to display and arrange them on the construction-paper backing. When you're happy with your arrangement, use hot glue to attach the pieces in place.

9. Fold the lid and window back into place, and you've got yourself a shadow box. Feel free to decorate the outside of the box if you like.

INTERVIEW: Collector Tom Eichhorst

Tom Eichhorst with a little bit of his collection

Collections and the lifelong learning that grows out of them begin in small ways. Tom Eichhorst is one of the world's foremost experts on the gastropods called nerites, but his interest began with some shells his grandparents bought in a tourist shop.

"My grandparents vacationed in Florida when I was seven and brought back a few shells for me in New Mexico. I thought they had picked up the shells on the beach, but later, after reading a few books and identifying the shells, I realized they were from the Philippines and my grandparents must have purchased them in a shell shop." It didn't matter: Tom was intrigued.

Initially, he simply glued his shells to a board for display and stored others in a shoe box. But as his collection grew and his interest developed, he wanted

to keep his shells where he could see them. He began displaying them in a cabinet, organized by family. His shell collection now fills many cabinets, as well as bins and storage boxes.

When Tom was in the eighth grade, he had a small aquarium with saltwater fish and a hermit crab. "I put a fighting conch shell (*Strombus pugilus*) in the tank, and sure enough, the crab moved out of the old shell he was living in, and into the conch shell."

A few months later, while feeding his fish, Tom saw what he thought was a dead hermit crab lying next to the conch. "I threw away the 'body' and put the conch shell on the shelf by the tank." That night he heard a crash. "I turned on the light and there was my conch shell on the floor with the hermit crab crawling out of it looking for

A hermit crab will make its home in any available shell.

A carrier shell complete with its collection of other shells

water!" The "dead body" that Tom had found was simply the crab's exoskeleton, which it had shed. The live crab was still living in the conch shell, waiting for its new exoskeleton to harden! "I put it back in the tank," says Tom, "and it thrived for quite some time."

When he first began collecting, the only information Tom kept was the name of the shell. "But one day when I was buying some shells," he recalls, "the dealer told me that I needed to keep better records. Unless I kept the data with the shell—such as where it's from, and where I found it or who I purchased it from, and when— it would only be a tourist curio and almost worthless to other collectors." From then on, he kept a slip of paper with each shell, recording the scientific name, the place where the shell was collected, when it was collected, and by whom.

Collecting shells teaches you about the natural world, but there are also lessons to learn about *protecting* the natural world. "I have learned that the greatest threat to mollusks and other sea life is pollution of our oceans," Tom says. "Raw sewage and chemical waste are still being dumped into the world's oceans at an alarming rate. There are a few shells that are illegal to collect in the wild or to sell, but that leaves about 50,000 shells that have been named that can be collected and another 150,000 shells that have not yet been named by science. We name about 800 new species each year."

Unless I kept the data with the shell— such as where it's from, and where I found it or who I purchased it from, and when— it would only be a tourist curio and almost worthless to other collectors.

Among Tom's favorite shells are "carrier shells" in the genus *Xenophora*. "These shells gather other smaller shells and rocks and attach them to their own shell as they grow. No one really knows why they do this."

Asked about advice for young collectors, he responds: "Limit your collection. If you try to collect just any shell, then the choices are so varied that you lose direction. Start with one family or one group or maybe shells from a certain area. You can always expand your collection later."

COLLECTING FOSSILS

WHAT ARE FOSSILS?

Fossils are the preserved remains of ancient life, and the study of fossils is called paleontology. (In ancient Greek, *paleo* means "ancient," *onto* means "beings," and *ology* means "the study of.") Just about any living thing, from dinosaurs to snails, from plants to pollen grains, has been found as a fossil. Even soft-bodied animals, such as jellyfish and protozoa, have left fossils. Ancient plants and animals have left behind their remains in stone, in amber (fossilized tree sap), and in natural tar deposits.

Nearly all fossils that are found in rock are found in sedimentary rock. It's formed when sediment, such as the sand and clay from glaciers, is compacted under heavy pressure. Moisture is squeezed out during the process, and the materials are compressed to become stone. This process is called lithification (*litho* means "stone"). If a plant or animal is buried in the sediment during lithification, it can become a fossil. Some familiar types of sedimentary rock are called sandstone, limestone, siltstone, and shale.

Ammonite fossils in limestone

BODY FOSSILS

Whenever any portion of an organism is preserved—such as bones, teeth, seashells, or parts of a plant—it is called a body fossil. These are among the most common types of fossils. In fact, when you think of a paleontologist uncovering the bones of a dinosaur, that's a body fossil. Some body fossils might have been buried and petrified (literally turned into stone; *petro* also means "stone") when minerals in the earth replaced the original organic material that the bones or wood were made of.

Natural *molds* are formed in stone when an organism is buried, but then dissolves or rots away during lithification (the process where loose sediments become stone). In that case, it will leave a mold of its exact shape in the stone. Natural *casts* are formed when the mold becomes filled with mud or other sediment, and then that becomes rock.

All sorts of plant and animal life have been found as fossils, including this fern.

Some fossils, like this Spinosaurus tooth, have been carefully removed from the rock they were imbedded in.

This amber-fossilized Jurassic scorpion didn't get to where it was going before it was engulfed in resin.

Discovering dinosaur tracks. Tracks like these are called trace fossils, because they leave a trace of the animal's behavior.

UNALTERED REMAINS

Unaltered remains are fossils that are preserved with little or no change. A whole mammoth preserved in ice, a Jurassic bug caught in amber, ice-age bones and beetles preserved in tar, or natural mummies are all examples of unaltered remains.

TRACE FOSSILS

Trace fossils are remains of behaviors, such as walking (tracks), digging (burrows), or pooping (coprolites). No part of the actual animal is preserved in a trace fossil. Some of the most spectacular trace fossils are dinosaur trackways, where footprints are preserved as natural molds or natural casts in sedimentary rock.

Burrows have been left by worms, rodents, and even burrowing clams or shrimp. Among the most interesting are burrows left by a shrimp called *Ophiomorpha*; these shrimp burrowed through the sand in shallow water, and then reinforced the tunnel walls with little balls of poop. When the now-fossilized burrows are exposed, they can look like little corncobs! Coprolites form when poop dries out and is then rapidly buried.

IDENTIFYING YOUR FOSSILS

One of the first questions anyone asks about a fossil they find is, "What is it?" There are many ways to get an answer, including studying books, checking with local museums, or visiting good websites.

Many natural history museums have staff members willing to identify fossils you might have found. If you can do so, make an appointment and when you go to the museum, make sure you have information that might help the paleontologist identify your specimen. One of the first questions they will ask you is, "Where did you find the fossil?" Follow our tips for keeping fossil records.

A limestone wall with fossilized sea life

HOW TO COLLECT

Fossil hunters and rock collectors are often called "rock hounds." Before going out to look for fossils, do a little homework. Because fossils are generally formed when an organism is buried in sediment, you will want to look for fossils in sedimentary rock, such as sandstone, limestone, or shale. Geologic maps are a wonderful tool—they will tell you where to find the right kinds of rocks. You can buy geologic maps at bookstores or online from the United States Geological Survey (USGS). The Roadside Geology series has a book for nearly every state, each with maps and stops for interesting geology, including places to find fossils. Computers are an excellent tool as well. A simple search for "fossil hunting in [your state]" will get you started.

SUPPLIES FOR COLLECTORS

Fossil collectors rarely dig for fossils: they keep an eye on surfaces. In deserts, coastal cliffs, caves, quarries, and other places with little ground cover, fossils can often be found on the ground or the surface of rocks. In areas with dense ground cover, road cuts (where a hill or mountain has been cut through to make space for a road) might be the only place anyone can see the inner surfaces of rocks. Here are some things to take along:

- A backpack makes carrying fossils much easier.

- Newspaper, re-closable plastic bags, or pill bottles to wrap and protect your discoveries.

- A rock hammer. These are sometimes called pick hammers and they have a pointed end to the head. If a fossil is in a large rock, you might need to use a hammer to break it free. Never hit the fossil directly with your hammer. It may be rock, but it can still break!

- Safety goggles—flying chips can be dangerous!

- Gloves—broken rock can have very sharp edges.

- Notebook. Keeping a notebook is a great way to record information on your finds. Some pieces of information you might want to keep are:

  - Where you found your fossil; sometimes that's a key to identification. Also, if you want to go back to where you found your fossil, your notes will remind you how to get there.

  - What kind of rock did your fossil come from? Each rock type is a clue to how the organism lived.

  - How common (or how rare) is it to find this type of fossil in the area where you were collecting?

  - When did you collect the fossil and who were you with?

  - Funny or interesting stories you would like to remember about your trip.

Most national parks don't allow fossil collecting, but they can be great places to look.

Be a Thoughtful Collector

Take time to learn what kinds of fossils you can legally collect and where you can collect them. The website www.gatorgirlrocks.com has loads of information on laws governing collecting. As a rule, on private property, the fossils belong to the people who own the land. Whether or not they allow fossil hunting on their land is up to them. Get permission from landowners if you would like to collect on their property.

Fossil hunting is allowed on some public lands, but not all. On national forest lands, collecting fossils of invertebrates (animals without a backbone) is allowed as long as it is for personal use and in limited amounts. Hunting for vertebrate fossils (animals with a backbone) requires special permits.

National parks, national monuments, national wildlife refuges, and wilderness areas generally do not allow collecting of any type of fossils without a special permit.

HOW TO CLEAN FOSSILS

Once you get home, you'll be ready to sort and clean your fossils.

1. Rinse with water. A gentle rinsing is fine for most fossils. BUT if your fossil is in siltstone or shale, don't use water: the siltstone might return to being silt, and the shale could once again become mud!

2. Scrub gently with a toothbrush to remove dirt and rock on more stubborn specimens. Always test a sample you won't mind losing before you scrub a fossil you really like—you might accidentally scrub the fossil off!

3. Etch with vinegar. In some limestone fossils, a sea creature's fossil shells have been silicified (replaced with quartz) and they can be cleaned by soaking them in vinegar. Here is a test to see whether a fossil has been silicified:

   a. Drip some white vinegar on the rock. If it fizzes, the rock is limestone.

   b. Drip a tiny drop of vinegar on the fossil. If it fizzes, STOP! The fossil is also limestone and will be ruined with vinegar.

   c. If there is no reaction, then the fossil is silicified, and can be cleaned with a vinegar bath.

   d. Use a bowl large enough to hold your fossil. Put the fossil in and add enough vinegar to cover.

   e. The limestone will fizz, indicating the acid is reacting with the rock. Keep an eye on your fossils as they soak.

Bubbles form on limestone when it comes into contact with vinegar.

   f. Let the rock soak for a couple of minutes.

   g. Remove and brush the fossil gently with a toothbrush. Be careful: some fossils that have been replaced with silicates are thin and fragile. Stop before the fossil becomes so brittle that it breaks.

   h. Rinse with fresh water to remove any remaining vinegar. Dry your fossil.

An old toothbrush and tap water are all that is needed for cleaning most fossils.

POLISHING

Few fossils need more than a cleaning to get them ready for display, but some can use a little touch-up. For hard fossils found in limestone, you can rub in a few drops of mineral oil. Oil will make the fossil stand out from the stone.

Fossils preserved in shale are best left clean and dry. Some sources recommend using varnish as a way to preserve fossils in shale, but varnish can shrink or expand depending on temperature. This shrinking and expanding can destroy the fossil!

Petrified wood chips can be polished in a rock tumbler. Tumbled wood can be very pretty and can be displayed as is or made into jewelry. Follow all directions carefully if you choose to use a rock tumbler.

A cleaned fossil

DISPLAYING AND STORING YOUR COLLECTION

Now that you have cleaned your fossils, you might be thinking of ways to display or store them. Rule number one: be creative! Here are a few suggestions to get you thinking:

- Riker mounts are glass-covered cardboard trays with cotton liners for cushioning and securing your specimens. They are handy because you can mount small or flat objects in the mounts and keep them on a desk, or hang them on a wall like a picture.

- Use interesting-shaped jars to display interesting fossils. Sort the fossils so each jar has one type. This can make a very nice display on a bookshelf or a desk.

- For anyone wanting to be more organized, craft stores sell clear plastic boxes used for sorting beads or buttons. These boxes are perfect for small samples. Put a label in each compartment with the name of the fossil.

- Many fossils are pretty enough to wear as jewelry. Wrap fossils with craft wire from a hobby supply store to make attractive pendants.

Riker mount frames can be used for shells, fossils, small rocks, and other collections.

The museum's fossil collection

STORAGE

A fossil collection can take over your house! Plan to store the ones that you don't need to have on display. Shoe boxes are great for fossil storage. Label each box with its contents so you can find your fossils quickly. Wrap your fossils in tissue paper or newsprint when you store them. They may be stone, but they can still chip!

Plastic shoe boxes are also excellent for storing fossils. If you stick with buying one type of box, they will stack neatly. Plastic boxes are also waterproof, so fossils that are in siltstone or shale will not be damaged if the box gets wet.

Cardboard trays and egg cartons are useful for holding small fossils if you are storing them in a cabinet or on shelves. If you want to keep a scientific collection, include a label with each specimen so that you'll remember the name and when it was collected.

KEEPING RECORDS

Often, as a collection grows, so does your curiosity. What kind of animal or plant was this? How did it live? How old is it? Where can I go to learn more? There are many ways to learn more, but some of it starts with sorting your fossils and with keeping records.

SORT YOUR FOSSILS

Decide how you would like to sort your fossils. You might sort by how the organisms are related (for example, all the snails together as a group), by where they came from, by the type (such as body fossil or trace fossil), or perhaps by size or color. The way most scientists sort their collections is by how they are related to one another or by where they came from.

One way to begin learning something about a type of fossil you've never seen before is knowing where it came from. Depending on the size, each fossil can be placed in a small cardboard box or re-closeable plastic bag, then all the specimens in a family can be kept together in a shoe box or plastic boxes.

Write a label for each specimen. The information you'll want to record includes the following:

- **Where** was the fossil collected? This is very important because it may help with identification.

- **When** was the fossil collected? Knowing when you collected the fossil turns your notes into a diary.

- **Who** collected the fossil? This becomes important as your collection grows and friends and family start giving you fossils.

- Notes include information you want to remember, along with more specific information on where your fossil came from. If you can, add its age and scientific name.

All of the fossils in this group are plants, gathered from the same area.

Project: Fossil Impressions

YOU WILL NEED:

- scissors

- package of modeling clay (we used Model Magic)

- fossil

- pencil

- pebbles or other things for making indented marks

- string or yarn

By using modeling compound, you can share an interesting fossil you found with a friend, or turn it into a pendant to hang on your wall or wear as jewelry. You can find modeling compound at any crafts store; it looks just like ordinary modeling clay, and it air-dries to a hard finish within 24 hours once you take it out of the package. Best of all, when you press a fossil into it— it makes a perfect impression.

1. Use the scissors to open the package of modeling clay. Pinch off enough to make one or two pendants. Tightly wrap the rest of the compound in the packaging or a plastic bag so it doesn't dry out.

2. Roll the clay between your hands. Flatten it on your work surface to a size and shape a little bigger than your fossil.

3. You don't want it too thin or it will be fragile when it dries—cookie thickness is fine.

4. Press the fossil firmly into the clay. If you want to turn your fossil impression into a pendant, leave some extra space around the border for a hole.

5. Lift the fossil out of the clay, and you have a perfect impression! (If you're not happy with the first impression, simply scrunch the clay into a ball again and start over.)

6

7

6. If you're making a pendant, decide where you want the hole to be. Use a pencil or another pointed tool to carefully poke a hole in the border.

7. If you like, decorate the border with small pebbles. You can remove the pebbles to leave impressions, or let them stay embedded in the border.

8. Place your impressed fossil on a flat surface to sit for 24 hours. When it's dry, thread a string through the hole and hang it or wear it and enjoy it!

FOSSIL HUNTER: Mary Anning

In the early 1800s, women's scientific discoveries and observations were not taken seriously. Yet, Mary Anning, who began fossil hunting as a child, persevered in her passion and became one of the world's foremost fossil hunters. England's Royal Society now considers her one of the ten British women who've most influenced the history of science.

Mary Anning was born in 1799 in the seaside village of Lyme Regis on England's southern coast. The cliffs there, facing the English Channel, are the country's greatest source of fossils from the Jurassic period (about 200 million years ago). Mary's father, Richard Anning, was a furniture maker and an avid fossil hunter. He taught Mary and her brother Joseph what to look for and how to identify fossils on daily journeys, on foot, along the cliffs and coastline. They sold the treasures they found at Richard's carpentry shop, but, sadly, he died when Mary was eleven years old. The family was left desperately poor and without an income.

That event made Mary serious about fossil hunting. She and her brother helped support the family by collecting and selling their Jurassic specimens to tourists. Tourists and collectors from London and Europe flocked to Lyme Regis as a resort in the summer, but the best time to look for fossils was actually in the winter, when fierce storms blew waves against the cliffs, revealing new layers of rock. Those weather conditions also meant that winter was a dangerous time of year to walk on the beach because whole sections of the cliffs could fall to the shore in a landslide. But that didn't stop Mary.

In 1811, Joseph located a 4-foot (122 cm) long skull, which he thought was a fossilized crocodile head. Mary continued to go back to the site and eventually

Mary Anning was only twelve years old when she uncovered the first complete *Ichthyosaurus* fossil in England. These late Triassic—and early Jurassic—period reptiles measured more than 6 feet (2 m) long.
Mary Anning Discovering the Ichthyosaurus at Lyme Regis in 1811. Lithograph after a painting by Charles Edmund Brock, British (1870-1938) / Private Collection / © Look and Learn / Bridgeman Images LLM2795554

The Jurassic coast of Lyme Regis where Mary Anning found her fossils

Mary was a very skilled observer of the fossils she found, making detailed drawings and keeping notes such as these describing a Plesiosaurus. Although she was self-taught, she knew more about Jurassic-period creatures than many of the "experts" of her day, because of her close and thoughtful observations on-site. It's the best way to learn. Pen and ink annotated drawing of a Plesiosaurus by Mary Anning, 1824. Plesiosaurus / Natural History Museum, London, UK / Bridgeman Images NHM1454859

discovered and uncovered the rest of the enormous skeleton, which she sold to a collector. The skeleton was eventually sold to London's British Museum, where it was named *Ichthyosaurus*. (The name means "fish-lizard.") It was the first complete *Ichthyosaur* specimen known, and Mary was twelve years old when she found it! She did not get credit for her discovery at the time—the collector she sold it to did!

She did not get credit for her discovery at the time— the collector she sold it to did!

By the time Mary was a young teen, Joseph had begun his career as an upholsterer, and she carried on alone. Although she did not have a proper education, she could read and write, and she kept detailed notes and drawings of the fossils she uncovered, which helped her compare the specimens she found and learn from them firsthand.

By studying on location, reading everything she could, and talking with the collectors and scientists who came to buy specimens from her, Mary became one of the most learned paleontologists in England in her day. All the same, as a woman, she was not allowed to participate in any of the scientific societies where ideas were discussed and discoveries were presented, or even to *visit* those societies when the fossils she had discovered were on view!

Although most men found it impossible to believe that a self-taught female was capable of knowing *anything* about science, there were a few who sought her out, particularly for her exceptional knowledge. These included the Swiss-American naturalist Louis Agassiz (1807–1873), the only scientist during her lifetime to name two fossils after her: *Acrodus anningiae* and *Belonostomus anningiae*—both of them fish.

Some of Mary Anning's important discoveries included the first complete Plesiosaurus, the first British example of a Pterosaur, and the skeleton of a Squaloraja. But the example she is still most known for is the *Ichthyosaurus* she found when she was twelve. In 2015, 168 years after her death, the species *Ichthyosaurus anningae* was named after her.

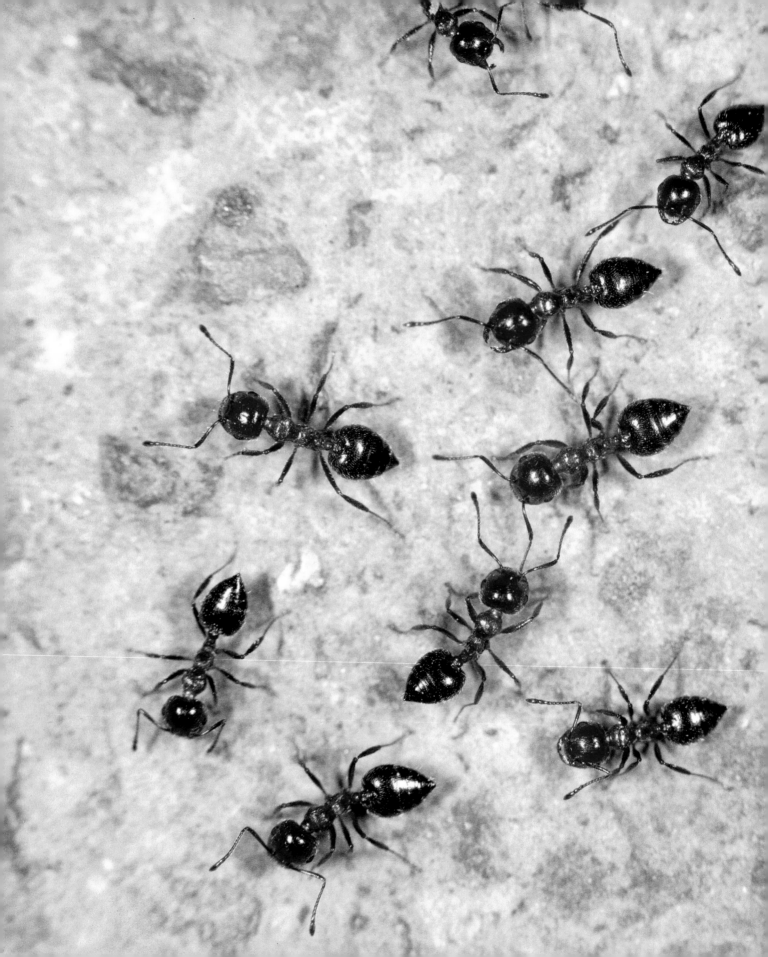

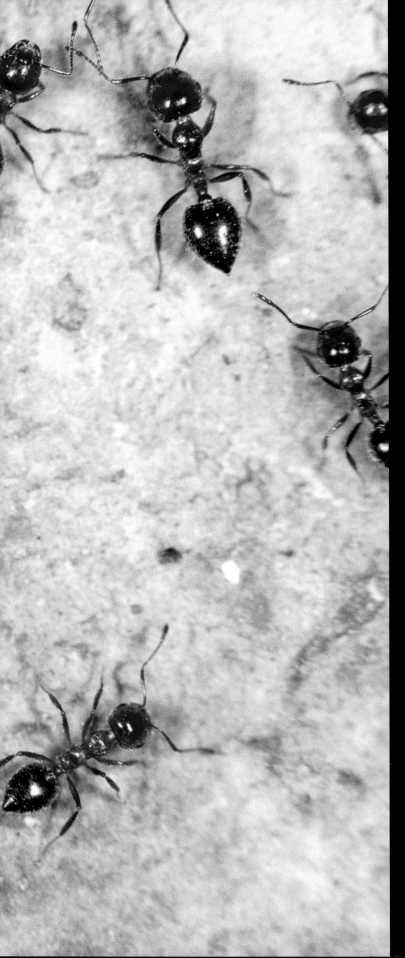

COLLECTING INSECTS

THE AGE OF INSECTS

We warm-blooded animals may think of this time period as the "age of mammals," but it is truly the age of insects—there are some 12,000 species of ants alone! Insects are everywhere—on every continent, warm or cold, even in Antarctica. Some thrive in wetlands, some in deserts, some burrow in the earth, some live in trees, and some may prefer the cool, dark recesses of your basement. If you're interested in insects, you'll find subjects to study for a lifetime.

Insects are only one class of a larger group of animals called Arthropods—any animal with an exoskeleton. These include the extinct trilobites, insects and springtails, spiders, scorpions, crabs, shrimp, millipedes, centipedes, horseshoe crabs, and sea spiders.

A Devonian-period trilobite, an extinct arthropod that lived 400 million years ago

WHAT DEFINES AN INSECT

So, what defines an insect within the category of Arthropods? All insects have three body segments—head, thorax, and abdomen. Starting with the head, most insects have compound eyes made up of many smaller eyes. Each eye has a lens, an optic nerve, and pigment cells. Dragonflies can have as many as 30,000 of these eyes, making two compound eyes that can see all the way around their heads! An insect's head also includes its antennae, for smell and touch, and its mouthparts, which can be adapted for chewing, sucking, or acting like a sponge.

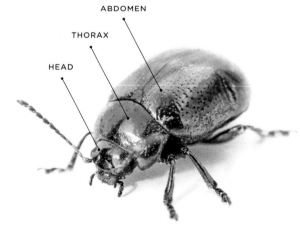

ABDOMEN

THORAX

HEAD

Green beetle

Close-up of the compound eyes of a horsefly (*Tabanus abdommalis*)

A fly has only two wings.

The thorax includes the insect's legs. Most insects have six legs, although there are exceptions to the number; monarch butterflies look like they have four, but taking a closer look you will see two tiny front legs. There are some adult insects that have no legs at all. If an insect has wings, they are located on the thorax. Most insects have four wings, but some, like flies, have only two. And there are wingless cockroaches, wingless wasps, wingless beetles, wingless moths, and even wingless flies!

An insect's abdomen contains all the vital organs, including the heart, reproductive organs, and digestive system. Insects do not have lungs; they breathe through holes called spiracles on the abdomen. Stingers on wasps, ants, and bees are modified egg-laying tubes; and beware—only females can sting!

Insect Orders

There are twenty-eight major orders of insects. The following are among the most familiar:

- **flies** (order: Diptera)
- **fleas** (order: Siphonaptera)
- **true bugs** (order: Hemiptera)
- **beetles** (order: Coleoptera)
- **dragonflies** (order: Odonata)
- **bees and ants** (order: Hymenoptera)
- **butterflies and moths** (order: Lepidoptera)
- **grasshoppers and crickets** (order: Orthoptera)
- **cockroaches and termites** (order: Blattodea)
- **praying mantis** (order: Mantodea)

Be a Caring Collector

Part of what's fascinating about studying insects is watching them in their habitats, going about their lives alone or in colonies. In bringing insects home to create a study collection, always remember that you are collecting living things. Only take as many insects as you need for your collection, and perhaps one or two more to trade with another collector.

IDENTIFYING INSECTS

One of the greatest challenges of collecting insects is identifying them. If you start by collecting larger insects, such as butterflies, grasshoppers, or large beetles, you'll find them easily in a field guide. Once you start to collect and begin to understand insects' life cycles and habits, you'll probably find one group more interesting than another. As this happens, your collection will become more focused. In the Resources section in the back of this book, you'll find a list of some of the best books to look at in the library.

Beetles, like this leaf beetle (*Gastrophysa polygoni*), have a hard wing cover.

Cicadas are true bugs.

BEETLES (ORDER: COLEOPTERA)

Nearly 25 percent (that's one out of every four) of all described animal species on Earth *are beetles*. With over 400,000 named species, and close to 1,500,000 suspected to exist, beetles are the most successful animals on the planet.

So, what makes a beetle a beetle? Most beetles have hard wing covers called elytra that protect the wings.

When a beetle gets ready to take off, its wing covers pop open, the wings unfold, and off it flies! All beetles have chewing mouthparts. All hatch from an egg, and go through a larvae (grub) stage, then a pupa (cocoon), and finally emerge as an adult.

The largest beetle in the world, the titan beetle, is almost 6½ inches (16.5 cm) long, and the smallest, a featherwing beetle, is only 0.0128 inch (0.33 mm) long and .004 inch (0.1 mm) wide. That is about as wide as a human hair!

TRUE BUGS (ORDER: HEMIPTERA)

For most people, anything with more than four legs is a bug, but not all "bugs" are *true* bugs!

True bugs, including "stink bugs," aphids, and cicadas, do not go through larvae and pupa stages like beetles. They hatch from their eggs as tiny replicas of their parents and just get bigger until they reach adulthood. All true bugs have sucking mouthparts. They can't chew or lap up their food; they have to pierce a hole in what they are going to eat with their tubular beak and suck fluids through it. It's a lot like poking a straw through the top of a juice box. Finally, the wings on most true bugs fold into an X pattern across their backs. So, if someone points to a beetle or a cockroach and calls it a bug, you know better!

The peanut bug looks a bit like a peanut.

Treehoppers are among the strangest-looking insects.

Another strange treehopper.

Not surprisingly, the scorpionfly has a tail like a scorpion's.

Strange Names and Weirder Looks

With so many species of insects, some are bound to look like nothing else in this world or to have a name that sounds like a joke.

For strange looks, consider scorpionflies, peanut bugs, and treehoppers. Scorpionflies look like someone glued a scorpion's tail to a fly and then added a tiny elephant's trunk to the head. Luckily, scorpionflies can't sting or bite. Some are known to eat small insects trapped on spider webs!

A tropical stick insect looks just like a stick.

WHERE TO LOOK

Ladybugs just after the rain

Remember that when you uncover insects in the wild, you're uncovering a creature's home. When you turn over a log or a rock, put it back as you found it—and keep your eyes on the task; there are many things out there that can bite, sting, or poke you!

Begin by looking in different habitats in your neighborhood. Gardens have different insects than a lawn, woods, ponds, or your home—and the variety of insects may change with the time of year. Some of them, such as leaf-litter mantids, walking stick insects, and dead-leaf butterflies, use camouflage to hide: *you may be looking straight at them before you actually see them*! Plan on collecting both during the day and at night; many species of moths come out only at night, and butterflies during the day. Look around your home—one study found that there were more than thirty different species of "bugs" in any home, at any time. You may want to check windowsills in your attic or basement for dead insects.

SUPPLIES

You can start collecting insects with very few supplies, but some of them make insect hunting much easier. Here are a few things you might want to have on hand.

Insect nets: If you've ever tried to catch a grasshopper, you'll know it's fun but challenging. If you are serious about collecting insects, then you will want a net. There are three types: aerial, sweep, and aquatic. Aerial nets have a long handle and are usually very light. These are used to catch butterflies, dragonflies, and other insects that fly away when approached.

Sweep nets are heavier, and usually have a shorter handle. These are strong enough to drag over grass and weeds without damaging the net and are perfect for catching grasshoppers and beetles. Aquatic nets have a strong cloth bag with netting attached at the bottom. These are made to drag through the water.

If you're just starting to collect, choose a net that has a light handle and a strong mesh bag. That way you can collect both flying and ground-dwelling insets.

Bed sheet: Use an old white or light-colored sheet that your family doesn't need anymore. You can use the bed-sheet method for collecting insects if you live in an area where there are lots of trees or shrubs. Spread a sheet out under a branch and give the branch a good shake. (Be careful not to break the branch!) Check the sheet and see what fell off the branch.

Medicine bottles: When you are out for a walk, take small, empty pill bottles in your pocket in case you find an insect you would like to collect.

Lights for night collecting: Many insects come out only at night. Other nocturnal insects will fly toward lights. To attract insects to your patio or door, swap out "warm white" light bulbs for "bright white" compact fluorescents. Hang or spread a white sheet under the light and watch as night-flying insects come to the sheet. Insects that make noise, like crickets and katydids, will immediately stop chirping as you get close. You have to be patient and stay very still until they either begin to sing or move around.

Short-handled nets are helpful for collecting crawling insects.

Nets for collecting insects from the air, by "sweeping," and from the water

Move the insects from your net to a jar.

INTERVIEW: Dr. Ayesha Burdett

Dr. Ayesha Burdett is the curator of biology for the New Mexico Museum of Natural History and Science. "As curator, I wear three hats," she says. "I do research, I'm involved with education and exhibits, and I oversee collections." How she became a curator, chose her field of study, and began collecting is an interesting story.

Ayesha grew up in the small farming community of Wickliffe, in the state of Victoria, Australia. "I didn't think of myself as very outdoorsy," she recalls, "although I actually did spend quite a lot of time outdoors, mostly by the river." When Ayesha was young she never really felt a need to collect from nature, because there was so much to be seen around her, but she cared very much for the environment and its inhabitants. She relates a story: "I went camping with my mother and some of my aunts; a cousin started to tear bark off a dead tree and I wanted him to stop because he was destroying a creature's home. My aunt told me I was 'such a greenie!'"

The Natural History Museum's Dr. Ayesha Burdett

Ayesha liked animals and thought about becoming a veterinarian . . . but soon learned she didn't like having to worry about "grumpy pups."

After high school, Ayesha decided to study at the University of Melbourne. She was good in biology. "Most smart kids who liked biology went on to become doctors," she recalls. But Ayesha liked animals and thought about becoming a veterinarian. She took a job working for a vet, but soon learned she didn't like having to worry about "grumpy pups." She also didn't like being indoors all the time. A summer spent as an intern at a hospital doing research seemed successful when she discovered an interest in parasites but, again, she found herself "going *mad* being in a lab all day long."

While still an undergraduate student, she went to the University of Washington in the United States on an exchange program, and took classes in social biology, entomology (the study of insects), and wildlife biology. For a short time, she became fascinated with ants, but she finished her degree with an honor's thesis studying freshwater invertebrates (animals with no backbones) in rice fields in Australia.

When Ayesha enrolled in Charles Sturt University for her doctorate she had to make a decision about what her special field would be. Bugs + water + outdoors = a Ph.D. in freshwater invertebrates! But to study aquatic bugs, and discover what was out there, she had to build a collection.

Dr. Burdett doing her fieldwork

She became interested in museums when she discovered her university had no resources for storing her research collection. What makes a museum a museum? Collections! A museum is like a library—each specimen is a source of information. Museums are also time machines: specimens from long ago can be studied, and, Ayesha says, "Someone in the future—someone you don't know—can look back through all your data, and all that information will still be available. Perhaps that person will learn something you never even thought of, do research using new technologies, and test new hypotheses."

Collections are also important to education and exhibits. When a specimen is used for either an educational program or an exhibit, "museums are valued as places to get accurate and accessible information." Anyone wanting to know where a specimen came from can find that information.

A museum is like a library—each specimen is a source of information.

For Ayesha, what is the value of starting a collection? "It's all about learning to love nature." She says, "If you learn to press flowers, but become a banker, you still have an appreciation for that flower!"

KILLING INSECTS

Killing insects is a necessary step if you intend to build a study collection. It's part of an entomologist's job. For insects such as beetles, grasshoppers, and true bugs, this can be done by placing the insect in a wide-mouth jar and then placing the jar in the freezer. This will kill them quickly.

For insects such as butterflies and moths that flap their wings and could damage them, you will need to prepare and use a killing jar. Killing jars contain a small amount of nail polish remover or rubbing alcohol that will kill an insect very quickly.

1. To make a killing jar, mix about ½ cup (60 g) plaster of Paris into ¼ cup (60 ml) water in a can or plastic container. Stir until the mixture has the consistency of pancake batter. Pour the liquid plaster into a jar and gently rock the jar so that the plaster settles smoothly. Leave the jar open and allow it to set up for a few days, until the plaster feels dry to the touch.

2. Pour a small amount of nail polish remover or rubbing alcohol onto the plaster—just enough so the plaster looks wet. Allow it to soak in. Pour off any excess. Scrunch up a piece of paper towel loosely and push it into the jar. The paper towel will keep insects from flapping their wings and trying to fly, and will keep them from touching the damp plaster.

3. Screw the lid on tightly and label it: BUG JAR, POISON.

4. When you catch an insect, quickly open the jar and transfer the insect from the net to the jar. Quickly close the lid. Do not shake the jar! It's a good idea to write down where and when you collected the specimen. Include the location as well as the habitat; for instance, "Mill's Park, oak tree." You might also add notes about the weather and your collecting technique. Keep the insects in the jar until you get home. You can pin your insects right away or move them to the freezer and work on them later.

MOUNTING AND DISPLAYING YOUR COLLECTION

An insect's muscles begin to shrink and dry out as soon as the insect dies. If you don't work with them right away, the exoskeleton becomes fragile and it can be impossible to keep legs or wings from breaking off when you go to pin and mount them.

There are several ways to soften an insect that has become too dry and fragile to work with. The first, the hot water method, will work with most insects *except* butterflies, moths, and others with fragile wings. The second, the relaxing box method, is safe for butterflies and moths and will work for all other insects as well.

HOT WATER METHOD

A soak in very hot water works well for softening super dried-out beetles. This method will also work for most any kind of insect *except* butterflies, moths, and insects with delicate wings.

If you use a coffee cup for this method, make sure it's one your parents will not miss: after soaking bugs in it, they will probably not want to ever use it again!

Bring water to a boil in a kettle and pour it into a cup. Allow the water to cool for just a minute, then drop your insects in. Let them soak for at least 5 minutes. Using tweezers, gently remove one insect from the water and try moving a leg. If the leg feels like it will break before it moves, drop it back in the water for another minute or two. Check again. When you can move a leg, it is time to take the insect out and pin it.

RELAXING BOX METHOD

This method is recommended for butterflies, moths, and insects with fragile wings, but it will work with any type of insect.

Set out a plastic storage box and line the bottom with a layer of paper towel. A couple of sheets should do the job. Pour just enough water onto the paper towel to moisten it. Pour a little disinfectant cleaner onto the towel as well. This will prevent mold from growing on your insects while they soften.

Cut two pieces of plastic screen to fit inside the box. Place the two layers of screen over the paper towel. Place your insects on the screen, so they do not touch the paper towel. Put the lid on the box and let your insects soak up humidity for a couple of days.

After two days, check the insects by trying to move a leg or wing; if the leg moves, it's ready to be pinned. If the bug is still stiff, cover the box for another day. Keep checking each day until the wings move. Insects should not be left in the box for more than a week—any longer and they will begin to rot.

Project: Pinning Insects

YOU WILL NEED:

- insect specimens

- Styrofoam block, cardboard, or balsa wood block

- insect pins

- foam block

- tweezers

- mounting board

- strips of wax paper ¼" to ½" (6–13 mm) wide and about 3" (7.5 cm) long

Insect mounting supplies, including mounting boards and pins

After your specimens have softened, it's time to get them ready for pinning, display, and storage.

You use mounting pins to hold insects in place in display cases. It's best to use specialized insect mounting pins for this purpose and not the straight pins that are used for sewing. Sewing pins are thicker than mounting pins and will create too large a hole in a specimen.

Mounting boards are available in wood, cardboard, and foam. They are designed with a groove running through the middle. The groove allows you to center the insect on its pin. Insect collecting supplies can be found online by typing in "insect mounting pins" and "insect mounting boards." Several online suppliers are listed in the Resources section in the back of the book.

Mounting pins hold insects in place.

Mounted butterflies with the wings held in place with wax paper strips

1. After an insect has been relaxed (see page 89), gently press it down on a block of Styrofoam, cardboard, or soft balsa wood. Push a pin through the thorax between the wings so that most of the pin's length sticks out from the underside of the bug. Pick up the insect by the top of the pin, and transfer it to a foam block. Use tweezers to uncurl the legs and use pins to hold them away from the body. Leave the pins in the block until the insect has dried. Once the insect has dried, you can transfer it to a storage or display box.

2. Pin a butterfly through the thorax and transfer it to a piece of mounting board, setting the body in the groove. Using flat tweezers, open one wing at a time and spread each wing flat on the board. Use a thin strip of wax paper to hold down the wing. Pin the wax paper strip to the board. Be careful not to push a pin through the wing. Use the tweezers to move the front wing forward and the hind wing back until you are happy with the way they are arranged. (If you use your fingers for this you might rub off the scales.) Do the same for the other wing. Use a wider strip of wax paper to hold down the ends of the wings to keep them from curling as they dry. Use a pin to position the antennae.

3. Allow the butterfly to dry completely before you transfer it to a display box. This might take anywhere from a few days to more than a week, depending on the humidity where you live.

CARING FOR YOUR COLLECTION

Once your specimens have been pinned and dried, keep them safe in a storage box. Any sturdy box with a tight-fitting lid will work. Cigar boxes, chocolate boxes, and greeting card boxes are all good for the job. Tight-fitting lids are necessary because—believe it or not—there are beetles that will eat your dried insects! Tiny dermestid beetles can very quickly eat a prize butterfly and leave nothing but their own shed larvae skins and frass (insect poop).

To display your collection, move your specimens into riker mounts, standard insect boxes, or glass-top storage boxes. If you want to display part of your collection in a pizza box shadow box (page 56), you will have to make a small change to the design. Cut a piece of a clean Styrofoam tray to fit inside the shadow box. Pin your specimens to the foam, and tape the box shut. This will keep out the dermestids. Never use mothballs in a box with Styrofoam—mothballs will melt the foam!

DEALING WITH DERMESTIDS

Inspect your collection regularly for dermestid beetles; the sooner you catch a problem, the less damage they can cause. The first sign of dermestids is a very fine, brown dust (their frass) on the bottom of the storage box. You may find active adults and larvae, but they are not as likely to be seen because they rarely leave the inside of the insect they are eating.

To kill dermestids, take the entire infected box and place it in the freezer for between three and seven days (longer is better). This will kill any adults. Take the box out of the freezer and allow it to warm for at least 24 hours. This will allow any eggs on the specimen hatch. Put the box back in the freezer (again, between three and seven days) to kill any beetle hatchlings. Repeat if necessary. Keep some dermestids for your collection!

Store your collection in boxes with tight-fitting lids and keep them out of the sun: many insects will fade if exposed to direct sunlight.

WHAT TO KNOW ABOUT BUYING INSECTS

As your collection grows, you might want to add some exotic insects that you can't find in your neighborhood. One way to get unusual specimens is to purchase them online.

BEFORE YOU BUY

Have your parents help you with your order. If you find something you want to buy, check the online store's rating. Don't buy from anyone who has poor ratings; you are more likely to get specimens that are not well packed or are damaged when they arrive.

Sometimes you will find just what you want from a store that has only a few reviews. One way to find out whether they might be a good source is to first buy something from them that only costs a couple of dollars. If it doesn't work out, no big deal, but if you find a new reliable supplier, you win!

Try to buy from someone in your own country. Overseas orders can take a very long time to reach you, and the cost of shipping can sometimes be as much or more than the specimen!

Always double-check the species name against what is shown online. Sometimes a specimen is misidentified and what you see is not what you expect!

Make sure your specimen comes with some information—not just the scientific name, but at least where it was found.

WHEN YOUR SPECIMEN ARRIVES

When your specimen arrives, it will be very dry. Be extra careful when unpacking the insect, and then use one of the relaxing techniques described on page 89 before you try to pin it.

When you mount or store your collection, each specimen should be tagged with any information you have gathered. Information should include the species, where it was found, when it was found, and who found it. Write or print the information on a piece of paper about ½" x ¾" (1.3 x 1.8 cm). Pin through the insect, then through the blank end of the tag, leaving room for the legs. Now you can pin the

Here's how to label a tiny insect like this flea beetle.

identified insect in its box. Some collectors like to add a tag with the family name under the information and what the insect was eating when it was collected.

For mounting very small insects, cut a triangle no more than ½" (1.3 cm) long from cardstock (index cards work great). Put a very small drop of white glue on the tip of the triangle, and carefully place the insect on the glue. Allow it to dry before you put it in your collection box.

Project: Make a Bell Jar for Display

YOU WILL NEED:

- masking tape
- clean, dry 2-liter soda bottle
- scissors
- circular piece of florists' foam slightly wider than the bottle
- craft glue
- sand
- dried flowers
- shells or pebbles (optional)
- insects

Glass bell jars get their name because, like a bell, they are open at the bottom and closed at the top. Bell jars are great for displaying your treasures because they allow you to admire what's inside from all angles, while keeping it free of dust. For this project, you'll make a bell jar from a soda bottle to display an arrangement of dried flowers complete with insects!

1. Set out all the materials on your work surface.

2. Use the masking tape to mark a cutting line all the way around the bottle, just before it starts to narrow at the top.

3. Carefully use the scissors to cut the bottle along the top edge of the tape.

4. Turn the bottle upside down to make sure the cut edge fits on top of the florists' foam.

5. Set the bottle aside. Cover the top of the foam with craft glue and spread it smoothly.

6. Sprinkle sand over the glue to cover it. (If you don't want to use sand, you can use dried leaves or moss.) Pour off the excess sand and allow the glue to dry thoroughly.

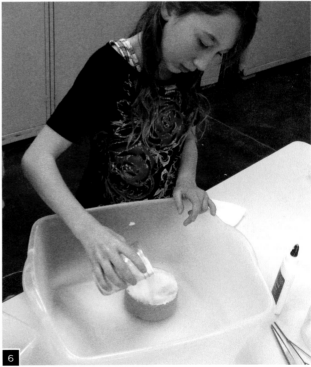

7. Make an arrangement of dried flowers, pressing them into the foam. Add shells and pebbles to the base if you like, and glue them in place.

8. Place the bottle over the flower arrangement to make sure the stems are the right height. Make the stems shorter if necessary and test them under the bottle again. When the height is right, set the bottle aside.

9. Arrange the insects on the flower stems and glue them in place. Allow the glue to dry.

10. Happy with your arrangement? Set the bottle on top and put the bell jar in a place of honor in your cabinet of curiosities!

COLLECTING PLANTS

START BY LOOKING LOCALLY

Collecting from the plant world is an enormous subject—there are some 600 species of oak trees alone! Fortunately for you, the plant world has fascinated people for a very long time, and they have written about it, photographed it, and made beautiful drawings to illustrate books. There are all kinds of field guides and books available to help you identify plants and to learn all about them.

Many books are specific to a category of plant—wildflowers or ferns, for instance. Some cover large territories, such as the trees of an entire country. Others zoom in and focus only on a single season, or a tiny corner of the world, such as the plants of a particular shoreline, mountain, prairie, or desert. Bookstores and libraries typically have a section for local or specialized books. Look in these sections for guides that interest you.

Once you begin looking, you'll discover that all plants change throughout the year, with some producing flowers or cones, and then producing spores or seeds. You'll also notice there is a time for new growth and leaves, and then a time for going dormant in the winter or dry season.

HOW TO COLLECT: PART 1

Start local! What interests you? Trees? Wildflowers? You have an exciting scavenger hunt ahead of you. Let's say your interest is wildflowers. Is there a wildflower that you pass by every day that you'd like to identify?

Make a few notes in your field notebook about the plant. What time of year did you notice it? Did it have flowers? Was the plant in full bloom? Where was it growing? What were the unique characteristics of its leaf shape and color? Take pictures of the plant's leaves and flowers and take your photos to the library. Then find a book that focuses on wildflowers in your area and try to find the one you photographed. Flowers might be the easiest way to identify a plant, but you can also identify it by its leaves and even its seedpods.

Found it? Read about it and make a few more notes in your notebook. What are the plant's scientific and common names? What kind of soil does it like? Does the book's description make sense with the place you found your plant? What else do you want to know about it?

Continue looking through the book and choose a couple more flowers you'd like to find. Perhaps you've seen them on your walks or in your yard but you never knew what they were called. Make new entries in your notebook for them and especially note what the book says about their habitat: Do they grow near streams? Do they like full sun?

This is where the scavenger hunt begins. Each time you find and identify a new wildflower, add it to your notebook with photographs and notes. You can do exactly the same thing with trees or any other type of plant. Once you've identified it, read about it and add to your curatorial knowledge.

Make notes about what kind of soil and habitat each plant prefers.

Leaves from different kinds of oak trees. The leaves, seeds, bark, and even the shape of trees will help you identify them.

Most plants that bloom in the spring will have fruit or seeds by late summer, and fall bloomers will have seeds that will not sprout until spring. There are some flowers, such as the evening primrose, that only bloom during the evening and some cacti only at night. Bottom line: be prepared to collect all year-round and both during the day and at night!

HOW TO COLLECT: PART 2

You can build your plant collection around the photographs and drawings that you make, or you can bring leaves, flowers, and other plant parts home for a hands-on study collection. We will show you several ways to press and dry your specimens so that they will last a long time.

THINGS EVERY COLLECTOR SHOULD KNOW

If you are going to be out looking for plants with the aim of bringing them home, carry a small pair of plant clippers or scissors in your backpack. Many stems and branches are tough and do not break cleanly when you try to pick them. Others have thorns or can cause skin irritations. Clippers will give you a clean cut and save your fingers.

Take cuttings that include some of the stem and leaves as well as the flower. The leaves are part of what identifies this forget-me-not.

Use clippers to cut branches and stems.

When you look for plants, bring a friend.

Be a Courteous Collector

With plants, as with all the collecting you do in nature, make sure you know whose property you are on when you take sample specimens. Get permission from landowners before you collect on their property, and never collect in wilderness areas. Only take what you need, and if you can only find a single plant, don't pick it!

Bring a few plastic bags in your kit to keep flowers fresh while you complete your collecting trip. An ordinary office folder can be handy for keeping leaves and ferns flat while they're in your backpack.

When you collect, pick enough of the plant to get both flower and some leaves; both will help you identify your plant. If you are collecting from trees, collect a small branch with leaves and, when they're available, flower clusters. Many fruit trees bloom very early in the season and the flowers begin to fall apart soon after. Collect and press them as soon as possible when the buds open to keep them in one piece.

Bring a friend! If you plan on going out and collecting plants or flowers, go with a friend or parent so you are not alone. An advantage to having someone with you is not only company, but also two sets of eyes will spot more interesting plants!

When you first begin a collection, you will most likely be collecting in your neighborhood, but as you get more involved, you might want to plan trips. There are many field guides that not only help you identify your plant but also give you an idea of where to look.

PRESERVING YOUR PLANT COLLECTIONS

Flowers, leaves, and other plants wilt, lose their color, and crumble as they age. How can you preserve plants so that you can look at them, learn from them, and enlarge your collection over time? Pressing or drying flowers, leaves, and plants allows you to keep them for a very long time. You can do this without having to buy special equipment.

PRESSING AND MOUNTING FLOWERS AND LEAVES

If you want to preserve the flowers, leaves, and other plants you collect in an album or in your field journal, you'll need to press them and then mount them on paper. We'll show you how to do both.

The best plants for pressing have delicate flowers—like daisies, buttercups, primroses, or snapdragons—or are thin, like leaves, ferns, and grasses. Thicker flowers, such as sunflowers and zinnias, don't flatten well and are preserved best by drying. Drying is covered in the next section.

The paper you use for mounting flowers and leaves should have a little bit of stiffness, so that it doesn't sag under the weight of the pressed plant and the glue doesn't cause the paper to pucker.

Project: Drying Delicate Flowers

Some flowers, such as lilies and more delicate roses, will wrinkle and lose color if they are air-dried. One way to prevent that from happening is to dry them in a mixture of borax and cornmeal. Borax, which is a mineral salt, will pull the moisture from the flowers. The cornmeal absorbs it.

Safety note: Have an adult help you with the Borax, which is used for laundry and other purposes. You can find it in the laundry section of supermarkets or hardware stores. Be sure to wash your hands after using it, and keep it away from your eyes. For this project, mix it with the cornmeal in a container that you can throw away or recycle, not a bowl that you use in the kitchen.

1. In the can or container, mix together equal parts Borax and cornmeal. You'll need enough to half-fill the shoe box.

2. Pour about half of the mixture into the shoe box, creating an even layer.

3. Place the flowers on top of the mix. You can place more than one flower in the box, but be sure not to let them overlap.

4. Gently sprinkle more of the borax-cornmeal mix over the flowers until they are covered with at least a 1″ (2.5 cm) layer.

5. Allow the flowers to remain in the mixture for a week or more, and then gently brush away some of the mix to expose a part of the flower. If it's dry to the touch, it's ready to come out. If it's still not completely dry, cover it again, and give it another week.

6. When your flowers are completely dry, carefully brush the mixture away and lift them out of the box. Your dried flowers are ready for display.

7. Store the borax-cornmeal mixture in an airtight container. Be sure to label the container with the ingredients and "FOR DRYING FLOWERS ONLY." When you are ready to reuse the mixture, spread it out on a disposable baking sheet and warm it to 150°F (65.6°C) for 30 minutes. Let it cool to room temperature.

YOU WILL NEED:

- can or container you can throw away

- Borax

- cornmeal

- shoe box

- flowers

- soft paintbrush

Project: Drying Thicker Plants and Flowers

Air-dry plants by hanging them upside down in a dry place.

YOU WILL NEED:

- fresh flowers or plants with stems

- rubber bands

- piece of heavy string or yarn, 2 yards (2 m) long

- dry, airy, and dark place to hang your flowers

- paper clips

Air-drying can be done with just about any plant, but it is a particularly useful technique for preserving thicker specimens like sunflowers, roses, and thistles, which will not respond well to pressing. If dried carefully, flowers will keep their shape and much of their color. If you have an attic in your house, that's the perfect place for drying plants. Choose flowers that are not quite in full bloom; after you pick them, they will open a bit more. Faded or withered flowers do not work well. Fresh is better!

1. Gather the flowers into small batches, not more than eight to ten stems per bunch.

2. Secure the stems of each bunch with a rubber band. Make sure the rubber band is tight, so the flowers won't fall out.

3. Fasten the string or yarn like a taut clothesline in an airy, dry attic or another dry space that doesn't get too much light. You can tie the ends of the string to two chairs and place the chairs far enough apart to pull the string tight.

4. Bend a paper clip to form an S-shaped hook. Hook one end of the rubber band on a bunch of flowers, and hang it on the string so that the flower-heads or leaves are upside down. Repeat as needed for each bunch of flowers.

5. Allow the flowers to dry for a couple of weeks. Once they are dry, remove the rubber bands and use the flowers in arrangements, as decorations, or as part of your plant collection.

Project: **Pressing Plants**

Creating a plant press is easy, but pressing flowers requires patience. Once your plants are inside the press, you will have to wait several weeks before you can enjoy the results. This allows the plants time to dry thoroughly while they are under pressure, which will prevent them from shriveling later. When you remove your plants from the press, they should be dry to the touch but still retain much of their color. Handle them gently.

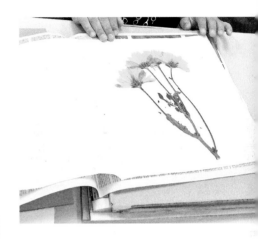

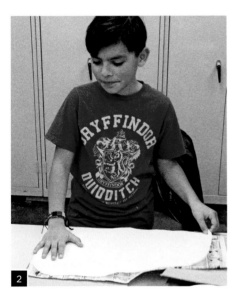

YOU WILL NEED:

- **2 sheets of cardboard cut to 10" x 12" (25.5 x 30.5 cm)**

- **newspaper**

- **paper towel**

- **flowers and leaves**

- **heavy books**

1. Building a plant press is like making a sandwich: you do it in layers. First lay down a piece of cardboard and place a sheet of newspaper on top of it.

2. Spread a piece of paper towel on top of the newspaper.

3. Carefully arrange your flowers on the paper towel.

4. Fold the paper towel over the flowers. Place a piece of newspaper over the towel.

5. Repeat steps 1 through 4, stacking the next layers on top of the ones you've already started.

6. Finish your stack with a sheet of cardboard on top.

7. Place heavy books on top of the stack—make sure the pile of books won't tip over!

8

8. Allow the plants to dry thoroughly. In dry climates, this might take a week or two; in more humid areas, it might take several weeks.

9. Test for dryness. Remove the books. Remove the top layer of cardboard and paper towel to see whether your plants have dried. If they're not dry, replace the towel, cardboard, and books, and give them another week. If they are dry, then they are ready to be mounted.

9

Project: **Mounting Dried and Pressed Plants**

YOU WILL NEED:

- newsprint or paper towel
- dried and pressed plants
- white glue
- 8½" x 11" (21.5 x 28 cm) piece of drawing paper or card stock
- index cards
- binder sleeves

Once you have dried your specimens using the correct technique for each type of plant, it's time to mount them.

1. Place a piece of newsprint on your work surface. Select one of the dried and pressed plants and decide which side of it you like best. Carefully place it good-side-down on the newsprint.

2. Squeeze a thin line of glue along the stem and the back of the plant.

3. Carefully center and place a piece of drawing paper over the plant.

6

7

4. Press the paper onto the plant, then gently flip it over. Allow the glue to dry.

5. Write your collection information on an index card and paste the card in one corner of the paper.

6. Place the sheet in a binder sleeve.

7. Store your pressed plants in a three-ring binder or album.

TIP:

If you prefer, you can use your pressed flowers and leaves to make framed pictures under glass or to decorate special gift cards.

PREPARING PINECONES

When you collect pinecones, collect some of the tree's leaves—its needles—too. Be sure to collect clusters of needles; each species of pine has a different number of needles per cluster. This will help you identify the tree.

Pinecones can be a problem because they are often homes for bugs, and they can be covered with sticky sap that will get on your hands and eventually all over the house. To address those problems, bake your pinecones when you bring them home, getting an adult to help you with the oven.

Pick off any needles, sticks, and larger globs of sap that are stuck to a cone's surface. Preheat the oven to 200°F (93.3°C). Spread foil on a cookie sheet. Place the cones on the foil and bake for 20 minutes. Remove the cookie sheet from the oven and allow the cones to cool. Any sap should have dripped onto the foil and will make less of a mess in your home.

Seed-bearing cones make an interesting collection because they come in so many shapes and sizes.

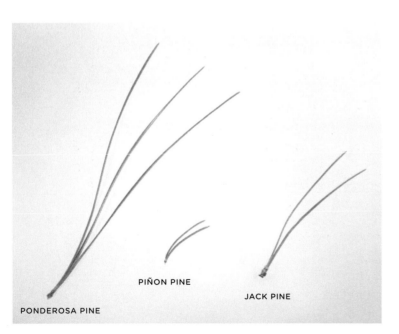

PIÑON PINE

JACK PINE

PONDEROSA PINE

Ponderosa pine, piñon pine, and jack pine needles. A tree's leaves, or needles, will tell you what kind of tree you are looking at.

Pine needles can be pressed and mounted like other leaves.

SORTING AND STORING YOUR COLLECTION

Sort and store your collection depending on how a plant was prepared.

Pressed flowers do not take up a lot of space and can be easily stored in a plastic sleeve in your three-ring binder. Each mounted specimen should have an index card pasted on it with the name of the flower and information about when and where it was collected.

Dried flowers can keep for a very long time but will crumble if they are not properly cared for. To protect your flowers from damage, place each in a cardboard or plastic storage box. Large flowers might need a shoe box. Store them in a closet or cupboard. Label each box with an index card.

The flowers in this antique album still have their bright color. Keeping dried flowers out of the sunlight will protect them.

Limber Pine   No: 177

Pinus flexilis   Date: July 8, 2017

Collector: Chris Anthemum

Where Collected: Watermelon mountains near charming dale

Habitat: Dry open rocky slopes above 7,000 ft.

ORGANIZING YOUR COLLECTION

There are many ways to organize your collection; here are three suggestions: (1) by color of flower, (2) by where the plants are found, or (3) by families. There are advantages to each way of organizing.

Color: Many books used to identify plants are divided by flower color. If you find a yellow flower, you don't have to go through the entire book to find your plant; all you have to do is look in the yellow section to begin your search. Keeping pressed flowers by color in your own three-ring binder is just like an identification guide.

Location: Another way to organize flowers in your binder is by where they were found. This method immediately identifies the plants of a particular neighborhood or a nearby forest or field.

Family: The third way is by family. As you get more familiar with plants, you will discover that roses, pears, and apples are all in the rose family; daisies and dandelions are "composites"; and peas, alfalfa, and peanuts are "legumes." This way of organizing your plants can have many surprises; who would think that Queen Anne's lace is related to carrots? When your collection gets large, you might have a separate binder for each family.

All of these flowers were found in the same spot. Organizing flowers by location will tell you a lot about their different needs and habitats.

Organizing flowers by color makes them easy to find.

Organizing plants by family, such as these rhododendron flowers, will help you develop a plant specialty.

Organize your field notebook and your collection any way that suits you—you're the curator and it's *your* cabinet of curiosities. Add to it, learn from it, share it, and grow with it.

ABOUT THE NEW MEXICO MUSEUM OF NATURAL HISTORY AND SCIENCE

Spending time at the New Mexico Museum of Natural History and Science allows visitors of all ages to explore a wide variety of natural history topics in a supportive and fun atmosphere. Become a paleontologist when you study fossils on exhibit. Travel deep into a volcano and discover the mineral riches of New Mexico. Blast off into space and explore the vastness of the universe in the Space Science wing and Planetarium or delve into a cave with bats and stalagmite formations.

The museum says its mission is to "preserve and interpret the distinctive natural and scientific heritage of our state through our extraordinary collections, research, exhibits, and programs designed to ignite a passion for lifelong learning. Our vision is to inspire a greater appreciation, understanding, and stewardship of science and our natural world."

Visit the museum in person at 1801 Mountain Road NW, Albuquerque, New Mexico, or online at www.nmnaturalhistory.org.

RESOURCES

BOOKS

There are many field guides for beginning and advanced natural history collectors. Below are just a few you might like to have in your collection.

Before you buy a copy, go to your local library or bookstore and look at all the guides available. Take your time looking at each, and then pick the one you like best.

A Field Guide to Animal Tracks (Peterson Field Guide Series) by Olaus Johan Murie, Mark Elbroch, and Roger Tory Peterson

A Field Guide to Insects of America North of Mexico (Peterson Field Guide Series) by Donald J. Borror and Richard E. White

Butterflies and Moths (A Golden Guide from St. Martin's Press) by Robert T. Mitchell and Herbert S. Zim

Fossils: A Guide to Prehistoric Life (Golden Nature Guides) by Frank H. T. Rhodes, Herbert S. Zim, and Paul R. Shaffe

Insects: A Guide to Familiar American Insects (A Golden Guide from St. Martin's Press) by Clarence Cottam and Herbert S. Zim

National Wildlife Federation Field Guide to Trees of North America by Bruce Kershner

National Wildlife Federation Field Guide to Wildflowers of North America by David M. Brandenburg

Rocks and Minerals: A Guide to Familiar Minerals, Gems, Ores and Rocks (A Golden Guide from St. Martin's Press) by Herbert S. Zim

Rocks, Gems and Minerals (A Golden Guide from St. Martin's Press) by Paul R. Shaffer and Herbert S. Zim

Seashells of the World: A Guide to the Better-Known Species (Golden Nature Guides) by R. Tucker Abbott

Wildflowers of North America: A Guide to Field Identification (Golden Field Guides) by Frank D. Venning

ONLINE RESOURCES

Insect Mounting Supplies

Bioquip
www.bioquip.com

Carolina Biological
www.carolina.com

Ward's Science
www.wardsci.com

Nasco Science
www.enasco.com/science

Fisher Scientific
www.fishersci.com

Naturalist Resources

www.inaturalist.org
A website where you can contribute to science by becoming a citizen scientist, or simply find out more about the natural world around you.

For Rock Collectors

The-Vug.com
www.the-vug.com/educate-and-inform/rock-and-gem-clubs
This website will help you find organizations in your area and connect with other collectors.

Gator Girl Rocks
www.gatorgirlrocks.com
A website both beginner and experienced rock hounds will find useful.

For Seashell Collectors

Conchologists of America, inc.
www.conchologistsofamerica.org
A great site for anyone interested in seashells. Links to local clubs, information, and more.

Hardy's Internet Guide to Marine Gastropods
www.gastropods.com
This website has thousands of photos of seashells.

ACKNOWLEDGMENTS

Thank you, Deb, for allowing me the opportunity and flexibility to work on this project. Kelly and Jayne, you not only read, edited, gave pep talks, and advised, but also picked up the slack while I was busy writing; thanks!

Anna, Ayesha, Mikayla, and Tom, thank you for granting interviews.

Thank you Addy, Amadeus, Benito, Beth, Caroline, Emily, Imogen, Juan Andres, Paloma, Tara, Zen, and Zia for your patience while being photographed, and your parents for allowing me the privilege of taking your pictures.

Alex: thank you for not only taking some awesome photos of activities, but also trusting me with your camera equipment. Ann: thank you for your help with props and setting up photo sessions.

Judith, many, many thanks to you for your guidance, patience, co-writing, editing, keeping the project on track, tracking down photos, dealing with my mistakes on the photo log … and the list goes on and on and on!

Special kudos must go to my wife, Kris, for your support and tolerating my working on this project at home, sometimes to ridiculous hours.

And last, but not least, thanks to all I may have failed to mention; the omission is not because of neglect, it's a result of so many who work in the background doing the kind of things that keep the wheels rolling!

ABOUT THE AUTHOR

Mike Sanchez is an educator at the New Mexico Museum of Natural History and Science. He has been interested in nature, "bugs," seashells, and dinosaurs from a very early age, and went on to get a degree in biological anthropology from the University of New Mexico. Mike loves to share his passion for the wonders of nature with people of all ages. His hobbies include collecting seashells (he began collecting when he was twelve years old), drawing, and scuba diving. He and his wife have two grown children and share their home with a really big dog named Tripp.

INDEX

To Kris, Alex, and Beth who contribute daily to my collection of best memories

Brimming with creative inspiration, how-to projects, and useful information to enrich your everyday life, Quarto Knows is a favorite destination for those pursuing their interests and passions. Visit our site and dig deeper with our books into your area of interest: Quarto Creates, Quarto Cooks, Quarto Homes, Quarto Lives, Quarto Drives, Quarto Explores, Quarto Gifts, or Quarto Kids.

Inspiring | Educating | Creating | Entertaining

© 2018 Quarto Publishing Group USA Inc.
Text © 2018 New Mexico Museum of Natural History and Science

First Published in 2018 by Quarry Books, an imprint of The Quarto Group,
100 Cummings Center, Suite 265-D, Beverly, MA 01915, USA.
T (978) 282-9590 F (978) 283-2742 QuartoKnows.com

Quarry Books titles are also available at discount for retail, wholesale, promotional, and bulk purchase. For details, contact the Special Sales Manager by email at specialsales@quarto.com or by mail at The Quarto Group, Attn: Special Sales Manager, 401 Second Avenue North, Suite 310, Minneapolis, MN 55401, USA.

10 9 8 7 6 5 4 3 2 1

ISBN: 978-1-63159-367-3

Digital edition published in 2018

Library of Congress Cataloging-in-Publication Data available

Design and Page Layout: Megan Jones Design
Photography: Shutterstock.com; except by Michael Sanchez on pages 10, 11, 12, 15, 23–28, 29 (top), 32, 33, 40–42, 51 (bottom), 60, 68–75, 80 (top), 85 (top right), 86–88, 91 (bottom right), 92 (top), 93 (bottom right), 94–99, 102, 109–115, 116 (bottom left), 120; Bridgeman Images on pages 8, 9, 14, 76 (bottom left), 77; Alex Sanchez on pages 56–59, and Bethany Sanchez on page 123.

Printed in China

MIX
Paper from responsible sources
FSC® C104723